new knits on the block

new knits on the block

a guide to knitting what kids really want

VICKIE HOWELL

PHOTOGRAPHY BY CORY RYAN

STERLING PUBLISHING CO., INC.
NEW YORK

Photography: Cory Ryan
Illustrations: Orrin Lundgren
Book Design: Vertigo Design Inc.
Project Consultant: Ellen Liberles
Proofreading: Eileen G. Chetti
Editor: Rodman Pilgrim Neumann

LIBRARY OF CONGRESS CATALOGING-IN-PUBLICATION DATA
Howell, Vickie.
 New knits on the block : a guide to knitting what kids really
want / Vickie Howell ; photography by Cory Ryan.
    p. cm.
 Includes index.
 ISBN 1-4027-2065-3
 1. Knitting—Patterns. 2. Children's clothing. I. Title.

TT820.H8132 2005
746.43′2041—dc22   2005010340

10 9 8 7 6 5 4 3 2 1

Published by Sterling Publishing Co., Inc.
387 Park Avenue South, New York, NY 10016
© 2005 by Vickie Howell
Distributed in Canada by Sterling Publishing
c/o Canadian Manda Group, 165 Dufferin Street
Toronto, Ontario, Canada M6K 3H6
Distributed in Australia by Capricorn Link (Australia) Pty. Ltd.
P.O. Box 704, Windsor, NSW 2756, Australia

Sterling ISBN 1-4027-2065-3

For information about custom editions, special sales,
premium and corporate purchases, please contact Sterling
Special Sales Department at 800-805-5489 or
specialsales@sterlingpub.com.

dedication

For Tanner and Tristan, my two favorite little rumpus makers.
I love you soooo much.

contents

acknowledgments

First of all I'd like to thank the Academy for nominating me for this honor. My performance would not have been possible without the support of your establishment . . . Oh wait, wrong speech.

But seriously folks, there are so many people responsible for this book's coming to fruition. I'd like to express my extreme gratitude to the following people:

Thank you so much to Sterling Publishing for giving me this amazing opportunity. You've made a dream come true for me. I'm especially appreciative of Jo Fagan for your patience and guidance from start to finish, Rodman Neumann and Ellen Liberlies for tediously combing through the copy and patterns to ensure that it all made sense, Karen Nelson, Jeannine Ford and the art department for making the book look great and being willing to take my suggestions into account, and Chris Vaccari and the marketing department for holding my publicity hand. You've all made my first publishing experience an absolute pleasure.

I'm deeply indebted to the yarn companies that supplied us with the great fibers for this book's projects and to Frank Stewart, who took time away from his big-name celebrity clients to work on a deal for little ol' me.

This book wouldn't be what it is without the amazing designs from its contributors. Your hard work, creativity, and brilliance make me so proud!

Cory Ryan, my friend and photographer, I feel so lucky that we were able to enter the book world together. You and I, along with our fantastic photo assistants, Karly Hand, Sarah Neff, and Stacey Simpson, made one awesome team!

To all of the wee models: thank you so much for bringing life to each project through your own faces and personalities. You're all beautiful, amazing kids.

The city of Austin did not disappoint when it came to finding places to shoot photography. I'd like to give a special shout out to Jennifer Perkins and Chris Boehk, Chia Guillory, Westgate Lanes, and Austin Fire Department's Station 6 (Thanks for suiting up, Daniel!) for opening up their places to our team. I really appreciate it!

On a personal note, I'd like to thank all of my family and friends who have supported me emotionally, spiritually, and psychologically. I owe so much to all of you, especially to the following: Clint Howell for always believing in me and for being the most amazing father to our children, Libby Bailey (my incredible mom) for being my number one cheerleader and greatest nurturer of the crafty gene, Kevin Montoya for being the one whose opinion I value most, Tammy Izbicki for being the keeper of my sanity and whose friendship is like air and water to me, Jenny Medford for your beautiful sarcasm and invaluable help with kid wrangling, Jennifer Perkins for constantly making me laugh, Kevin Iudicello for ensuing hilarity when I most needed it, with your witty life commentary, Emma Gibson for your late night grammar wizardry, Whitney Lee for our "work days," the Austin Craft Mafia for inspiring me never to stop creating, Bev Galeskas and Candi Jensen for showing me the knitting ropes, Kelly Mooney for her mad brainstorming skillz, Alessandra Ascoli and the gang at Screen Door Entertainment for opening up doors for me that I had before only dreamed of, the Knitty Gritty crew for always taking such good care of me, Stitch 'n' Bitch Austin for encouraging me to get my "knit on," the MEOWers (especially Karen Baumer for her "Fancy Pantsiness," and Lori Steinberg and Susan Gould for lending me their knitting hands), who, through thick and thin, always make me feel as if I have support nationwide, and lastly, Tanner and Tristan, whose boundless spirits re-create life for me every day. I love you all.

mikey likes knit

I grew up, for the most part, in the 80s. Like most children, when it came to gifts, I had a couple of well-meaning relatives who brought me useful items like underwear, socks, and classic books. Although I never would've expressed my disappointment, clearly, I was less than thrilled by their gestures. I mean, what does an elementary-school-aged kid care about practicality? I would've much preferred E.T. shoelaces, a Cabbage Patch doll, an Oingo Boingo tape, or a New Kids on the Block poster (I mention the latter at the risk of losing any street cred I may've had). Sometimes the life of a six-year-old is so unfair!

Well, here it is twenty-plus years later and the tables are turned. I'm a parent who also happens to be a knitter, and as much as I enjoy stitching scarves, sweaters, and mittens for the pint-sized men in my life, their reaction to my efforts mirrors my own lack of excitement when I was in their shoes. Alas, what's a crafty mama to do?

If I've learned anything in this life, it's that compromise is key. If one plan of action doesn't work, then it's time to approach the situation from a different angle. So, I got to thinking, how could I apply this same philosophy to my current knitting dilemma? I needed to find a happy medium between my own love for working with yarn and my children's insatiable desire for toys. The result was the creation of this book. The twelve amazing contributors and I really tried to step out of the box by designing patterns for everything from a superhero cape and bowling set to mermaid and Viking costumes. The following pages offer twenty-five super-original, funky playtime projects that are as much fun to knit as they are to receive. There's a new knit on the block, people, so sit back, relax, and enjoy the wild ride!

don't leave home without knit!
tips for busy knitters

People are always asking me how I find time to knit while chasing around after two small children and working on various jobs. Well, it's simple. I don't sleep. Ever. Nah, I'm just kidding. With a little planning, it's possible for even the busiest person to bring creativity into one's life, no matter what form it takes. Since I'm a knitter obsessed, here are my ten tips for fitting your knit into your day.

1. If you're really short on time, be realistic with your project choices. Pick something quick and easy to knit up so that you don't get frustrated by the lack of progress.

2. Whether it's English or continental, choose the method of knitting that proves speediest for you.

3. In general, working with slick, lightweight metal needles and clean (non-novelty) fibers are quicker to knit with. The stitches glide off the needles nicely and it's easier to catch any mistakes if there aren't extraneous yarn bits masking your knittin' and purlin'.

4. Keep a small project in your bag or car so that when you find yourself waiting in line at the DMV or sitting at the doctor's office, you can use that time to knit. After all, craftiness is the best cure for the irritation one is sure to feel during life's time-sucking obligations.

5. Bring your project to your child's soccer practice, dance rehearsal, or art class, and knit from the sidelines.

6. Trick your kids into (ahem), I mean, encourage your kids to hold the book and turn the pages while you read them a story and work on your project. That way you're having quality kid *and* knit time all at once. Multitasking = good.

7. If you carpool or ride public transportation to work, bring your knitting along. Knitting in places like the subway is a great way to pass the time!

8. If possible, join or start your own Stitch 'n' Bitch group (aka knitting circle). This ensures that even if it's only for one evening a month, you'll have time on your calendar set aside solely for craftiness.

9. Teach your kids to knit. If your kids are sitting around knitting, then you can be too!

10. Knit in bed. Although your partner may not be thrilled with this suggestion, knitting while watching a little nighttime TV is a great way to wind down from a busy day.

abbreviations & terms

beg = beginning

BO = bind off

CC = contrasting color

ch = chain

CO = cast on

dec = decrease

dpn(s) = double-pointed needle(s)

inc = increase

k = knit

k2tog = knit 2 stitches together for right-slanting decrease

k2tog tbl = knit 2 together through back loop

M1 = make one stitch (increase) by lifting connecting strand between last and next stitches onto left needle and knitting through the back loop

MC = main color

p = purl

pm = place marker

p2tog = purl two stitches together

rem = remaining

rep = repeat

rnd = round (a row worked around on a circular needle)

RS = right side

sc = single crochet

sl = slip

sl-w-t = slip, wrap, turn

ssk = slip, slip, knit (slip 2 stitches, one at a time as if to knit, then knit them together through the back loop for left-slanting decrease)

St st = stockinette stitch (alternate between knit and purl rows)

st(s) = stitch(es)

tbl = through the back loop

WS = wrong side

wyif = with yarn in front

wyib = with yarn in back

yo = yarn over

* or ** = (asterisk or double asterisk) marks starting (and, sometimes, ending) point to repeat instructions

rep from * = repeat all the instructions following the asterisk as many times as indicated, in addition to the first time

work even = work in pattern without increasing or decreasing any stitches

yarns used in projects

If you are unable to find the specific yarns and colors used in these projects at your local yarn source, you should be able to mail-order sources online. Simply search by the yarn manufacturer's name.

time after time

PROJECT LEVELS

All of the projects in this book are absolutely realistic for any beginning to intermediate knitter to give a try. As a parent, I'm always more interested in the amount of time that I'll need to invest in a project rather than the level of skill required. For that reason, the designs you'll see over the next pages aren't rated by difficulty level but instead by how long it'll take before you can answer the kid in your life's inevitable question, "Mo-o-om (or Auntie, Uncle, Grandma, Grandpa, etc.), is it done yet?!"

Playdate: Super quick to knit.

Weekend at Nana's: Moderately quick to knit.

Summer Camp: Takes a wee bit more time to knit, but is totally worth the wait.

it's the little things...
EXTRAS TECHNIQUES

I-CORD

With double-pointed or circular needle, cast on stitches. Knit across row. Once that row is complete, slide stitches to the opposite end of the needle and switch hands so that the needle (or needle tip, if you're working with a circular needle) with the knitted row is now in your left hand. The working yarn will appear to be at the wrong end of the row, but just bring it behind the stitches and begin knitting again. The strand of yarn stretched across the back will bring the stitches together to form a tube or cord. Continue in this manner until you achieve the desired length.

TWISTED CORD

Cut yarn length about six times longer than desired finished length of cord. Fold yarn in half and loop the folded end over a doorknob or other hook. Hold the two yarn ends taut and begin to twist them, turning the cord to the right over and over until it begins to twist back onto itself. Release the ends and the cord will twist itself into a cord. Knot the ends and trim.

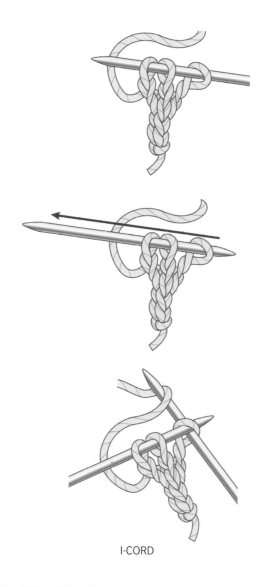

I-CORD

DOUBLE-STRANDING WITH ONE BALL OF YARN

If a project calls for using a double-strand of yarn but doesn't require the yardage of more than one ball, then simply pull a strand from both the middle and the end of the ball and hold them together as if one strand. Or pull out a clump of yarn from the middle of the ball and cut it off (you can wrap it into a neat separate ball of yarn if you prefer). Working from completely separate sources makes it less likely that your yarns will become tangled. To knit, hold the two strands (one from each source) together and knit as usual.

TASSELED FRINGE

Cut a cardboard rectangle ½ inch longer than the desired fringe length. Wrap the yarn loosely around and around the length of the cardboard. Cut the strands at one end and remove the cardboard. Select three to five strands, depending on how full you'd like your fringe to be; fold them in half. Insert a crochet hook from back to front through the edge of your project and catch the folded end and pull it through the edge to form a loop. Bring the cut ends of the yarn through the loop and tug on them gently to knot the loop at the edge of the project. Trim the yarn ends evenly.

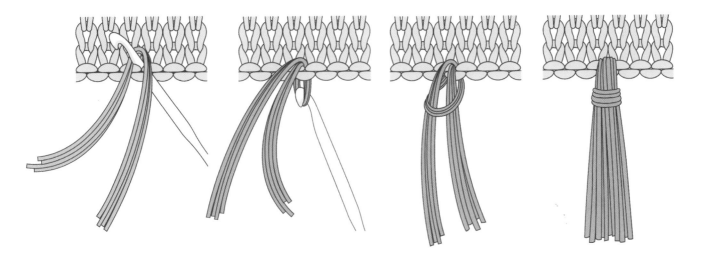

extras techniques

NEEDLE FELTING
(as told by the master, Bev Galeskas)

Place a piece of foam (at least two inches thick) inside the project under where you want the first design (for example, the star for the wizard hat). Begin by using small amounts of roving to form a rough shape of a star (or whatever shape you choose), stabbing with the size 38 felting needle to hold the fibers in place. Shape edges by pushing and pulling the fiber into place then stabbing with the needle, adding more fiber as needed. At this point the design is still easily removed if you wish to make changes. Once you are happy with the look, use the felting needle to attach the design permanently by stabbing (needling) repeatedly over the entire surface. Continue needling until the fiber is firmly attached to the felt.

HAND FELTING

Fill a bowl or pot halfway with water as hot as your hands can stand it. Add about of tablespoon of mild soap. You can use one of the fancy detergents made especially for wool or just use your own shampoo. Completely submerge your project in water and agitate by rubbing with your hands. Don't be afraid to be a little rough! Continue in this manner until fibers have merged together to your liking. Rinse soap out with cool water. Place project on towel, shape as necessary, and let dry.

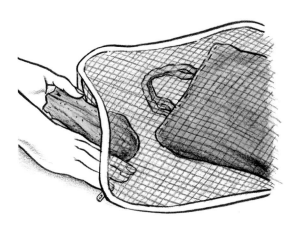

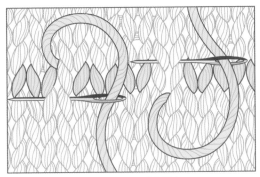

DUPLICATE-STITCH

MACHINE FELTING

Place knitted project in a zippered pillowcase or finely meshed bag. Throw bag into the washing machine along with an old pair of jeans or towel (this will help with the agitating process) and wash item on hot, being sure to exclude the "spin" portion of the washing cycle. Repeat as many times as necessary to achieve desired felting result. Take care to check on your project every five minutes or so. When finished, squeeze excess water out of project, shape per pattern instructions, and let dry on a towel. Keep in mind that felting will work only with natural, animal fibers that *have not* been "superwash" treated.

DUPLICATE STITCH

Duplicate stitch is used to embroider a design over knitted fabric. Use a tapestry needle and yarn that's the same weight or slightly finer than the piece was knitted with. Bring the needle up through the bottom of the *V* of the knit stitch to be embroidered. Insert needle under both loops of the stitch above the one you're duplicating, pull yarn through, and take the needle back down through the point of the *V* where you started.

MATTRESS STITCH

Mattress stitch is used to seam side edges of the knitted pieces together neatly. Lay the two knitted pieces to be seamed on a table, side by side and right side up. If you stretch the edge of one piece gently, you'll see a row of yarn strands between the stitches (like the rungs of a ladder). You will work up these rungs as you join the sides. To stitch, anchor the yarn on the wrong side and bring the tapestry needle, threaded with matching yarn, up from the wrong side at the bottom edge of one piece. Slide the needle under the next rung and draw the yarn through. Stitch under the corresponding rung on the other knitted piece. Work back and forth in this way, climbing up the ladder, one or two rungs at a time, on each side of the seam. You'll notice that the edges draw together, creating an almost seamless seam. Work to the top of the seam and securely weave in ends.

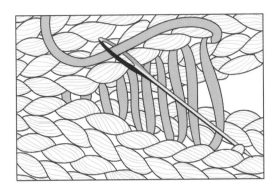

BACKSTITCH

Backstitch is used for embroidering lines. With yarn and tapestry needle, come up through your project at point A. Go back down with needle at point B, up at point C, and then down again through point A. For next stitch, come up through point D, and back down again through point C. Continue in this manner for as long as you'd like your embroidered-line embellishment to be.

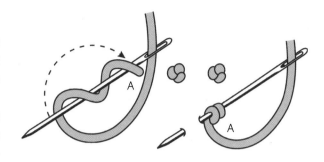

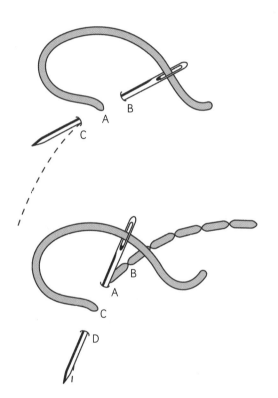

EMBROIDERED CHAIN STITCH

With yarn and tapestry needle, come up through your project. Holding down yarn with left thumb, insert needle from front to back through the same hole where you started. Before you pull the yarn through however, you'll need to go under and then up through, about a stitch and a half of your knitted piece. As you begin to pull the yarn through, you'll notice a loop forming. Come through that loop with your needle and then go back down at the same point that you just came up at to anchor the top of the loop. Continue in this manner.

FRENCH KNOT

French knots are used to make raised dots. With yarn and tapestry needle, come up through the point (A) in your knitting where you'd like your French knot to be. Wrap yarn around needle twice. Go back down near the hole (A) that you started from (but not the same spot), and pull so knot is created.

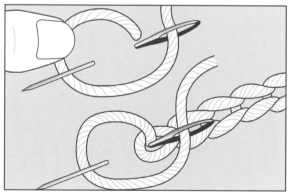

CROCHETED CHAIN

Make a slipknot on crochet hook; this will act as your first stitch. Wrap yarn over the top of the hook, catching it with the end of the hook, and pull the yarn loop through the stitch on the hook. Continue in this manner until your chain is the desired length.

SINGLE CROCHET EDGING

Make a slipknot on crochet hook. Insert hook into front loop of knitted-edge stitch that you'd like to embellish. Wrap yarn over the top of hook, catching it with hook end, and draw yarn loop through the edge. You now have two loops on your hook. Wrap yarn over hook once more and draw through both loops on hook. One single crochet stitch is completed. Insert hook into next knit stitch. Wrap yarn over hook and draw through the edge (2 loops on hook). Wrap yarn again and draw it through both loops to complete another single crochet stitch. Continue in this manner until edging is complete.

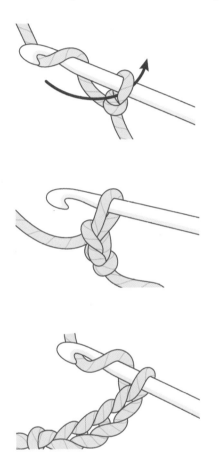

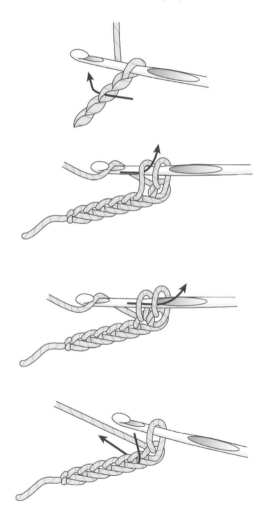

crafty tip

It helps to hold the tail of the yarn securely between your thumb and middle finger while you're working!

extras techniques

HALF DOUBLE CROCHET EDGING

Following instructions above, single crochet in first of your knitted-edge stitches. Next, wrap yarn once and insert hook into next knitted stitch. Wrap yarn and draw loop through edge of work. You'll now have 3 loops on your hook. Wrap yarn again and draw through all 3 loops. Continue in this manner until edging is complete.

DOUBLE CROCHET EDGING

Following instructions above, single crochet in first of your knitted-edge stitches. Next, wrap yarn once and insert hook into next knitted stitch. Wrap yarn and draw loop through edge of work. You'll now have 3 loops on your hook. Wrap yarn and draw through the first 2 loops (2 loops now remain on hook). Wrap yarn again and draw through these 2 remaining loops to complete double crochet. Continue in this manner until edging is complete.

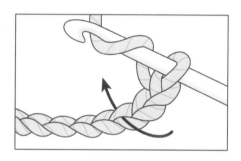

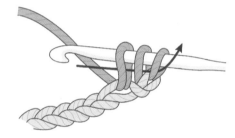

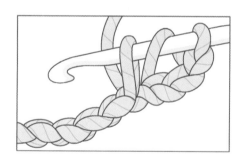

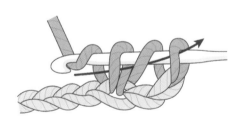

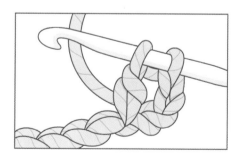

knit-tested,
mother-approved
projects

st. elmo's fire
firefighter hat

NATALIE WILSON FOR IKNITIATIVE, LLC • LEVEL: *weekend at nana's*

My children, ages three and five, love pretend-play, and Firefighter is one of their favorite games. They regularly build fire engine playscapes from boxes and chairs, and "borrow" my wrapping-paper rolls to use as fire hoses. With this felted hat, the fun continues on the playground and through the winter. Thanks to clever short-row construction, the hat can be worked in one piece. Easy-but-snazzy appliqué and embroidery complete the authentic look.

MATERIALS

yarn

Cascade 220 (100% wool; 220 yd per 100g skein):

1 skein Color 8895, Christmas Red (MC)

I skein (or small amount) Color 7826, California Poppy (CC1)

1 skein (or small amount) Color 8887, Dark Lavender (CC2)

needles

24-inch circular needle, US Size 10 (6mm) *or size needed to maintain correct gauge*

1 set (4) double-pointed needles (dpn), US Size 10 (6mm) *or size needed to obtain gauge*

1 pair straight needles, US Size 5 (3.75mm)

notions

Yarn needle

Tapestry needle

Tailor's (marking) chalk

Stitch markers

GAUGE

Before felting: 15 sts and 20 rows = 4 inches in stockinette stitch using circular needles

SIZE

One size fits most children ages 2 to 5 years old.

FINISHED MEASUREMENTS

Circumference: 20 inches

There is some flexibility to make the hat a little larger or smaller, depending on how severely or lightly the item is felted.

SPECIAL TECHNIQUES

short rows

Short rows are worked to add an extra number of rows to lengthen and shape a section of knitting; the work is turned before the entire row is completed. To make the turn invisible, a stitch is slipped and wrapped before turning.

To slip, wrap, and turn (sl-w-t): St st, bring yarn forward, sl st back to left needle, turn work, bring yarn forward. On the next regular (complete) row, pick up wraps as follows: Insert right needle tip through the wrap, then through the next stitch and work the wrap and stitch together as one.

knit-on cast-on method

To add stitches already on needle, knit the first stitch and keep original stitch on left needle; slip the new stitch onto tip of left needle (1 st added to left needle). Knit through the new stitch (closest to needle tip), keeping it on the left needle; slip newly made stitch onto left needle (another st added to left needle). Continue in this manner, knitting through last stitch onto left needle, until you have added the desired number of stitches.

directions

REAR FLAP EXTENSION

With circular needle and MC, CO 45 sts. Working back and forth (do not join), k 9 rows.

Begin short-row shaping: Next row (RS): K 21, sl-w-t. Next row (WS): K. Next row: K 19, sl-w-t. Next row: K. Continue as established, working 2 sts fewer before sl-w-t on each RS row until row with K1, sl-w-t and following k row are completed. Next row (RS): K across all sts, picking up wraps. On next row (WS) rep short-row shaping, beg with K21, sl-w-t. (Short rows worked on WS rows; k back on RS rows.) When shaping is completed, k across all sts, picking up wraps (45 sts).

COMPLETE BRIM

CO 71 sts onto end of needle using knit-on cast-on method (116 sts). Pm on needle to mark beg of rnds and join sts into a rnd. P 1 rnd, k 1 rnd, p 1 rnd. First dec rnd: K48, (k2tog, k5) 9 times, k2tog, k3 (106 sts). K 7 rnds even. Second dec rnd: K48, (k2tog, k4) 9 times, k2tog, k2 (96 sts). K 12 rnds even. Third dec rnd: (ssk, k8, k2tog) 8 times (80 sts).

CROWN

K 38 rnds even. Shape crown, changing to double-pointed needles when necessary:

Rnd 1: (k4, k2tog, k4) 8 times (72 sts).

Rnds 2, 4, 6, 8, 10, 12, 14, and 16: K.

Rnd 3: (k7, ssk) 8 times (64 sts).

Rnd 5: (k3, k2tog, k3) 8 times (56 sts).

Rnd 7: (k5, ssk) 8 times (48 sts).

Rnd 9: (k2, k2tog, k2) 8 times (40 sts).

Rnd 11: (k3, ssk) 8 times (32 sts).

Rnd 13: (k1, k2tog, k1) 8 times (24 sts).

Rnd 15: (k1, ssk) 8 times (16 sts).

Rnd 17: (k2tog) 8 times (8 sts).

Cut yarn and draw end through remaining 8 sts to close.

FINISHING

Felt hat (see page 14).

Once hat has been felted to your desired size, shape hat and lightly stuff it with plastic grocery bags to define the shape. Allow the hat to dry completely.

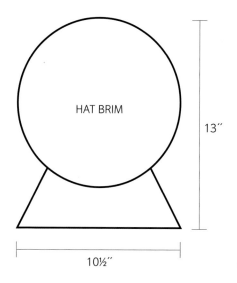

st. elmo's fire: firefighter hat

CROWN EMBROIDERY

With marking chalk, mark a line from center front to center back over crown. Mark two more lines evenly spaced along each side of this line. Mark a line around base of crown. With poppy (CC1) and yarn needle, embroider chain stitch (see page 16) along marked lines.

PATCH

With straight needles and lavender (CC2), CO 25 sts. K 3 rows. Row 1 (RS): K. Row 2 (WS): K3, p19, k3. Rep Rows 1 and 2 for 7 times more. Dec row (RS): K3, ssk, k to last 5 sts, k2tog, k3. Next row (WS): K3, p to last 3 sts, k3. Rep last 2 rows until 17 sts remain. Work Dec Row. K next row. Work Dec Row. BO knitwise on WS. Using single strand of poppy (CC1), embroider "F.D." on patch using backstitch. Center patch on front of hat just above embroidery at base of crown. Sew patch to hat with lavender (CC2).

swamp thing
monster hats

VICKIE HOWELL · LEVEL: *playdate*

These hats need no explanation. They're crazy and simple to make. Best of all, the kids dig 'em so much, that they'll actually keep them on during the cold weather. Well, maybe.

yarn

Crystal Palace Squiggle (100% new wool; 135 yd/125m per ball), 2 (2, 3) balls of Fern Mix OR Code Pink (MC) AND

Crystal Palace Shimmer (100% new wool; 135 yd/125m per ball), 1 ball Deep Green OR Strawberry (CC)

needles

1 pair US Size 8 (5mm) straight needles *or size needed to maintain correct gauge*

Crochet hook Size F (3.75mm)

notions

Sewing needle

Sewing thread to match yarn color

Tapestry needle

Sew-on "googly" eyes (see Crafty Tip, facing page)

~~~~~~

GAUGE

18 sts = 4 inches in MC and garter stitch (knit every row)

SIZES

6–18 months (2–4, 6–8 years)

directions

With CC, CO 34 (38, 40) sts. Work for 6 rows in k1, p1 rib. Cut CC.

Next row: Join MC and knit all rows until piece measures 12 (12½, 13½) inches. Cut MC.

Next RS row: Join CC and work in k1, p1 rib for 5 rows. BO in ribbing.

FINISHING

Weave in yarn ends. Fold piece in half so rib edges meet at bottom; sew seams at sides.

Measure in from top corner 2½ (2½, 3) inches and pinch fabric together. Wrap thread around fabric several times and tie off, creating an ear. Repeat process on other side.

Sew on googly eyes just above hat brim and as close together as possible (they will spread apart when hat is worn).

With CC and using a size F crochet hook, crochet 6 separate 12-inch chains (see page 17).

Tie three chains each around ears to create hanging swamp gook.

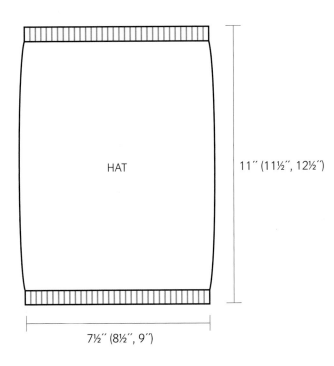

HAT

11″ (11½″, 12½″)

7½″ (8½″, 9″)

crafty tip

Because of the nature of the fabric that's been created with the novelty yarn, glue-on googly eyes don't work very well for this project. If that's all you're able to find at your local craft store, however, go ahead and buy them but also purchase a set of flat-topped shank buttons that you can glue the eyes on to. Let them dry, sew the buttons onto your hat, and your swamp thing's ready to give its not-so-icy stare!

swamp thing: monster hats

labyrinth
felted wizard & princess hats

BEVERLY GALESKAS   ·   LEVEL: *weekend at nana's*

Felting is a bit like magic, so it was a natural choice for these Felted Wizard and Princess Hats. No well-dressed wizard or lovely princess should be without a proper hat. I hope you will have as much fun knitting and felting these as I did working on the design.

MATERIALS

yarn

Worsted-weight wool (see Note), 280 yards for solid-colored hat OR

215 yards of main color and 65 yards of contrast for the 2-color hat.

note: Choose a yarn that will felt firmly so that hat will hold its shape. The model hats shown were worked in Lamb's Pride worsted from Brown Sheep Co. Always test felt your yarn before beginning a project.

needles

16-inch (40cm) circular needle, US Size 10½ (6.5mm) AND

1 set (4) double-pointed needles (dpn), US size 10½ (6.5mm), *or size needed to maintain the correct unfelted gauge.*

notions

Plastic ring for stitch marker

Tapestry needle

For Wizard Hat only: Small amount of gold or yellow fiber

Star-shaped cookie cutter for template (optional)

Felting needles

Piece of thick foam to work on

note: Fiber Trends' Needle Felting Starter Kits, which contain 4 needles and foam, are available at yarn stores.

For Princess Hat only: ½ yard of sheer fabric for veil

~~~~~~

UNFELTED GAUGE

13 sts = 4 inches (10cm) in stockinette stitch. Change needle size if needed to maintain this gauge.

FELTED GAUGE

(Will vary with the amount of felting) 16 to 18 sts = 4 inches (10cm).

SIZES

Will fit head sizes from 20 to 22 inches.

directions

BASIC HAT

Begin with bottom rolled band.

note: Use contrast color for 2-color hat or main color for solid-color hat.

With circular needle, loosely cast on 72 sts.

Join to work in rounds, being careful that stitches are not twisted around the needle. Pm on needle for beg of rounds.

Knit 3 rounds even.

Round 4: *K6, M1; repeat from * around (84 sts).

Knit 3 rounds even.

Round 8: *K7, M1; repeat from * around (96 sts).

Knit 3 rounds even.

Round 12: *K8, M1; repeat from * around (108 sts).

Knit 5 rounds even.

Round 18: *K1, k2tog; repeat from * around (72 sts).

Round 19: Knit.

If you are making a 2-color hat, cut contrast and join main color before continuing.

BODY OF HAT
Round 20: *K4, M1; repeat from * around (90 sts).

Knit 22 rounds even.

SHAPE TOP
Round 1: *K16, k2tog; repeat from * around (85 sts).

Knit 7 rounds even.

Round 9: *K15, ssk; repeat from * around (80 sts).

Knit 7 rounds even.

Round 17: *K14, k2tog; repeat from * around (75 sts).

Knit 5 rounds even.

Round 23: *K13, ssk; repeat from * around (70 sts).

Knit 5 rounds even.

Round 29: *K12, k2tog; repeat from * around (65 sts).

Knit 5 rounds even.

Round 35: *K11, ssk; repeat from * around (60 sts).

Knit 5 rounds even.

Round 41: *K10, k2tog; repeat from * around (55 sts).

Knit 4 rounds even.

Round 46: *K9, ssk; repeat from * around (50 sts).

Knit 4 rounds even.

Round 51: *K8, k2tog; repeat from * around (45 sts).

Knit 4 rounds even.

Round 56: *K7, ssk; repeat from * around (40 sts).

Knit 4 rounds even.

Round 61: *K6, k2tog; repeat from * around (35 sts).

Knit 4 rounds even.

Round 66: *K5, ssk; repeat from * around (30 sts).

Knit 4 rounds even.

Round 71: *K4, k2tog; repeat from * around (25 sts).

Knit 3 rounds even.

Round 75: *K3, ssk; repeat from * around (20 sts).

Knit 2 rounds even.

Round 78: *K2, k2tog; repeat from * around (15 sts).

Knit 1 round even.

Round 80: *K1, ssk; repeat from * around (10 sts).

Cut yarn, leaving a long tail.

crafty tip

Needle felting is definitely an interesting and most unique method of embellishing this project, but as an easy alternative, simply buy some craft felt, cut out several stars, and sew them onto the already felted Wizard Hat.

FINISHING

wizard hat

Using tapestry needle, thread yarn through the remaining 10 stitches, pull together tightly, and fasten off. Weave in all yarn ends. Now you're ready to felt (see page 14)!

princess hat

Using tapestry needle, thread yarn through the remaining 10 stitches. To create a hole in the top for the fabric veil, use your finger to hold the center open and pull yarn until the stitches are snug around your finger. Fasten off, taking care to leave the hole open. Weave in all yarn ends.

Machine felt (see page 15). Important: If making a princess hat, be sure to check that the hole at the top is staying open while felting, poking open with your finger, if needed.

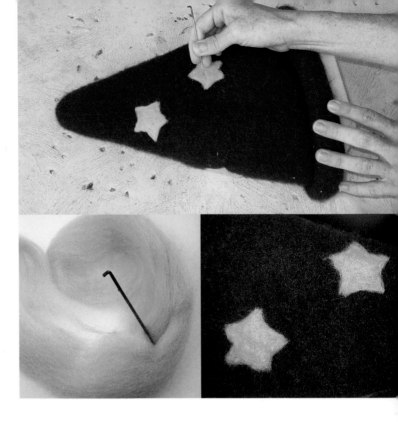

FINISHING

Pull into shape, rolling the lower band up. The lower part of the hat can be blocked over a bowl or ball just slightly larger than the recipient's head size. If the top looks as if it could use some blocking to smooth it, you can use a plastic bag filled with fiber-fill to mold the hat around.

When dry, brush lightly if needed to remove any clumps of wool.

NEEDLE FELTED STARS

First, decide on placement and mark each spot where you want a star with a pin.

Stars may be free-formed, or use a small star cookie cutter to trace around the shape.

Using the basic needle felting instructions on page 14, needle felt each star in place.

VEIL FOR PRINCESS HAT

Cut a piece of fabric about 18 by 20 inches. Pink or make a narrow hem around the edge if fabric ravels easily. Take one corner and push it through the hole at the top of the hat.

Pull enough fabric inside to allow a knot to be tied, then pull on the outside of the veil to tighten the knot up into the top of the hat.

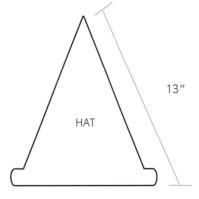

13"

HAT

20" (22") circumference

fresh prince
bejeweled crown

KAREN BAUMER • **LEVEL:** *weekend at nana's*

Children seem to love wearing the paper crowns they acquire at fast-food restaurants or make for themselves, so I decided to design a more permanent version. You can increase the amount of embroidery to make a truly opulent crown—or keep it simple and use the leftovers from the Lurex Shimmer to trim a purse or pair of gloves!

MATERIALS

yarn

Rowan Harris Tweed DK (100% pure new wool, 124 yd/113m per 50g ball):

2 balls Color 001, gray mist (MC) AND

Rowan Lurex Shimmer (80% viscose, 20% polyester, 104yd/95m per 25g ball):

1 ball Color 332, gold (CC1)

1 ball Color 333, pewter (CC2)

1 ball Color 331, claret (CC3)

needles

1 pair of straight needles, US Size 5 (3.75mm), *or size needed to obtain correct gauge*

16-inch circular needle, US Size 6 (4.25mm), *or size needed to obtain correct gauge*

notions

Straight pins

Tapestry needle

Polyester fiberfill

GAUGE

5½ sts and 8 rows = 1 inch in MC and stockinette stitch on smaller (straight) needles

SIZE

One size fits most 2- to 5- year-olds.

FINISHED MEASUREMENTS

21 inches circumference by approximately 5½ inches high at points (see note at end for making crown smaller or larger)

directions

CROWN

note: Crown is worked sideways in rows running from top to bottom of crown.

CROWN LINING

With straight needles, CO 15 sts.

Row 1 (WS) and all following WS rows: Purl.

Row 2: To begin shaping point at top, CO 2, k to end.

Repeat these two rows until there are 27 sts on needle, ending with a WS row.

Next row (RS): BO 2, k to end.

Continue to BO 2 sts at beg of every RS row until 15 sts remain, ending with a RS row.

Repeat from Row 1 6 more times.

BO all sts on WS row purlwise.

crafty tip

As an alternative to adding the beautiful embroidery to this crown, grab yourself some sequins or beads and sew them on in gemstone patterns. It's a quick, inexpensive way for this project to be royally bejeweled.

fresh prince: bejeweled crown

OUTER CROWN

Make same as for lining, but add charted texture patterns, alternating between charts A and B.

FINISHING

Block each piece. Sew each piece into a round using mattress st along short edges.

With right sides together and with back seams matching, sew zigzag edge together using backstitch (see page 16); turn right side out and stuff lightly with fiberfill. (You may want to lightly steam press the crown before stuffing.) Use a narrow, blunt-ended object (such as a large knitting needle) to poke out the crown's points completely. Stuff the points first, then the band, pinning the bottom closed as you go along to hold the fiberfill in place.

With double strand of pewter (CC2) and circular needle, pick up approximately 5 sts per inch all around the bottom edge of the crown, picking up sts through both layers of fabric to join them together.

Knit 5 rows of garter st, remembering that garter stitch in the round is P 1 round, K 1 round. BO all sts loosely.

Embroider squares and diamonds on crown with gold (CC1) and claret (CC3), using texture patterns as guidelines.

note: Can also be made for 18- or 21-inch head circumference by leaving off one section (for a total of 6 sections = 18 inches) or adding a section (for a total of 8 sections = 21 inches).

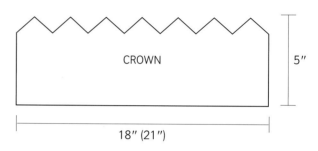

CROWN

5"

18" (21")

CHART A

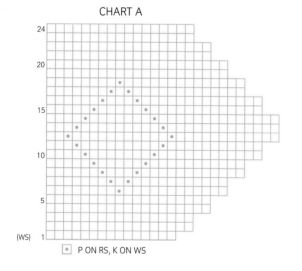

(WS)

· P ON RS, K ON WS

CHART B

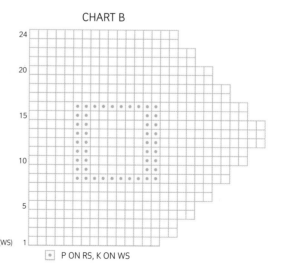

(WS)

· P ON RS, K ON WS

schneider
tool set & pouch

VICKIE HOWELL • LEVEL: *playdate*

When we're building or fixing something in our house, the kids always want to "help" by grabbing all of the tools. In effort to keep sharp metal objects out of their hands, I designed a softer set that they can hold in their own personal tool belt. Although it's doubtful that they'll stop going after the real thing any time soon, at least they'll look extra-cute doing it!

MATERIALS

yarn

Berroco Suede (100% nylon, 120yd per 50g ball):

1 ball Color 3714, Hopalong Cassidy tan (MC1)

1 ball Color 3717, Wild Bill Hickock brown (MC2) AND

Berroco Cotton Twist (70% mercerized cotton, 30% rayon, 85 yd per 50g ball):

1 ball Color Stone gray (CC)

needles

1 pair each of straight needles, US Size 4 (3.5mm), and US Size 6 (4.25mm), *or size needed to maintain correct gauge*

notions

Tapestry needle

Polyester fiberfill

Child-sized belt

GAUGE

20 sts = 4 inches on larger needles

FINISHED MEASUREMENTS

Tool Pouch: 6 by 8 inches

Saw: 8 by 3 inches at widest point

Screwdriver: 9 by 2½ inches at widest point

Mallet: 9 by 5 inches at head

crafty tip

As you stuff each tool, also insert a small dowel or plastic canvas piece to cut down on tool floppiness.

directions

TOOL POUCH

With brown (MC2) and larger needles, CO 40 sts. Work in St st for 11½ inches, ending with a k row.

Next WS row: Knit (this creates fold line for hem)

Work in St st for ½ inch. BO.

FINISHING

With WS facing you, fold up hem, then fold over edge an additional 1½ inches to create belt loop. Seam.

With RS facing you, fold up bottom edge 4 inches and seam up sides. Create individual pockets by sewing a straight line from bottom to top edge of large pocket, 2½ inches from left edge. Sew another line 2½ inches from the last line.

TOOLS (MAKE 1 OF EACH)

mallet

With tan (MC1) and smaller needles, CO 12 sts. Work 8 rows in St st.

Next row (RS): Ssk, k to last 2 sts, k2tog (10 sts).

WS: Purl.

Repeat last 2 rows once (8 sts).

Join in gray (CC) and work in St st for 1½ inches.

Next row (RS): CO 9 sts, K across.

WS: Purl. CO 9 sts across.

RS: K9, work next 6 sts in k1, p1 rib, K9

WS: P9, work next 6 sts in k1, p1 rib, P9

Repeat last 2 rows until piece measures 8½ inches. BO in St st and rib (at center).

screwdriver

With MC1 and smaller needles, CO 8 sts. Work 2 rows in St st.

Next row: K1, M1, k to last st, M1, k1 (10 sts).

Continue to work even in St st until piece measures 3½ inches.

Next row (RS): Ssk, k to last 2 sts, k2tog (8 sts).

WS: Purl.

Repeat last 2 rows twice more (4 sts).

Join in CC and work even until whole piece measures 8½ inches.

Next row (RS): Ssk, k2tog (2 sts).

WS: Purl.

BO.

saw (side one):

With MC1 and smaller needles, CO 17 sts. Work 6 rows in St st.

Next row (RS): BO 13 sts, k4.

WS: Purl.

Work 6 rows in St st (open area of handle formed).

Next row (RS): CO 13 sts, k across (17sts).

WS: Purl

Work 4 rows in St st.

Join in CC. Work 4 rows in St st. Shape saw edges as follows:

Next row (RS): Ssk, k to last 2 sts, k2tog (15 sts).

WS: Purl.

***RS (dec row):** Ssk twice, k to end (13 sts).

WS: Purl.

RS: Repeat last dec row (11 sts).

WS: Purl.

RS (inc row): K1, M1 (twice), k to end (13 sts).

WS: Purl.

RS: Repeat last inc row (15 sts).

WS: Purl.

Work 2 rows in St st.**

Repeat from * to ** once more.

RS: Repeat dec row (13 sts).

WS: Purl.

Repeat last 2 rows once (11 sts).

Work 4 rows in St st. BO.

With MC1 pick up 4 sts at outer edge of bound-off sts on open end of handle.

Work 6 rows in St st. Seam top edge to outer edge of cast-on sts at open end of handle, leaving an opening at center of handle.

jaw (side two):

CO 17 sts. Work 7 rows in St st.

Next row (WS): BO 13, P4.

Work 6 rows in St st.

Next row (RS): K4, turn and CO 13 sts (17 sts).

Work 5 rows in St st.

Join CC. Work 4 rows in St st.

Next row (RS): Ssk, k to last 2 sts, k2tog.

Next row: Purl.

*****RS (dec rows):** K to last 4 sts, k2tog twice.

WS: Purl.

Repeat last two rows once.

RS (inc rows): K to last 2 sts, M1, k1.

WS: Purl.

Repeat last two rows twice more.

Work 2 rows even in St st.**

Repeat from * to ** once more.

Repeat (dec row, p row) twice.

Work 4 rows in St st.

BO.

With MC1 pick up 4 sts at open end of handle. Work 6 rows in St st and attach as for first side. Seam edge.

FINISHING

With WS together, seam front and back of tool pieces. Leave an opening to stuff. Generously stuff each tool; sew opening closed.

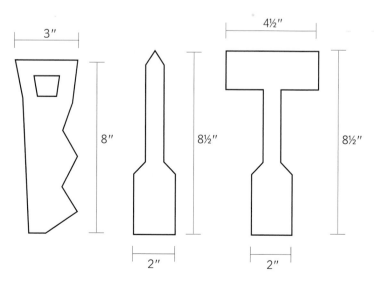

the tooth is out there
alien tooth fairy pillows

VICKIE HOWELL • **LEVEL:** *weekend at nana's*

Losing a tooth is a big deal in a little kid's life. Make saying "bye-bye" to baby teeth an out-of-this-world experience with these cool Alien pillows! Oh and when your child asks you if there's such a thing as the Tooth Fairy, just tell him or her not to worry; the tooth is out there.

yarn

Filatara Di Crosa 501 (100% new wool, 137yd/125m per ball):

Both versions:

3 balls (MC) (Dark Gray).

2 balls of desired face color (CC) (Lime Green)

1 ball of black (CC1)

(Girly version only): 1 ball of desired color (CC2) (Hot Pink)

needles

1 pair straight needles, US Size 6 (4.25mm), *or size needed to maintain correct gauge*

notions

Scraps of felt: black for pocket, pink for girly-version hair bow

12- by 12-inch pillow form

Sewing needle and thread

Tapestry needle

GAUGE
18 sts and 24 rows (MC doubled) = 4 inches square

FINISHED SIZE
12 by 12 inches

directions

FRONT

With 2 strands of MC held together (double-stranded), CO 54 stitches. Work 6 rows in St st.

note: To read chart, read right to left on RS rows and left to right on WS rows.

Next Row (RS): K10, with CC work 34 sts of chart, k10.

Next Row (WS): P10, with CC work 34 sts of chart, p10.

Repeat last 2 rows until all 66 rows of chart are finished.

Work 5 more rows of MC in St st. BO.

BACK
CO 54 sts. Work in St st for 77 rows. BO.

mama tip

If your child plans on resting his or her weary head on this pillow while awaiting the tooth fairy's arrival, be sure to put the tooth into a baggy before placing it into the pocket. This will ensure that the "chomper" won't slip through the knitted stitches and get lost in the pillow's stuffing.

I-CORD PIPING

Using double-stranded CC or CC2 (for girly version), CO 3 sts. Knit 48-inch I-cord (see page 12). BO.

FINISHING

Block front and back pieces.

Using CC1 and following chart, duplicate stitch alien eyes and nose onto the face.

Create tooth pocket by cutting out small piece of black felt in desired mouth shape and hand sew onto alien's face, leaving top of mouth pocket open. If you're making the "girly" version, cut out a bow-shaped piece of pink felt and hand sew onto the alien's head.

With wrong sides facing and using mattress stitch (see page 15), sew the front and back pieces of pillow together along 3 edges, leaving the top seam open. Insert the pillow form and sew the top seam.

Following the seam line, pin I-cord piping around pillow and then hand sew onto pillow using sewing thread.

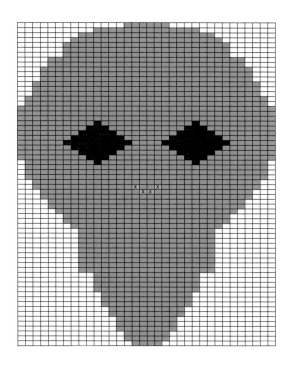

X duplicate stitch in CC1

goonie's treasure
pirate bath set

LORI STEINBERG • LEVEL: *summer camp*

I wanted to design something for this book, and a friend suggested a pirate costume. I immediately thought of an eye patch, a head scarf, a Jolly Roger, and a parrot. I love the washcloths I've made out of cotton chenille, so when I saw the crisp, bright colors available, I got the idea that the Jolly Roger would be a cool washcloth, and if I stuffed the parrot with a sponge, the whole thing would be a really neat bath set.

yarn

Crystal Palace Cotton Chenille (100% mercerized cotton; 98 yd per 50g ball):

2 skeins Color 9598, black (MC1)

2 skeins Color 9784, red (CC1)

1 skein Color1058, white (MC2)

1 skein Color 4043, green (MC3)

1 skein Color 9660, violet (CC2)

needles

1 pair of straight needles, US Size 6 (4.25mm), *or size needed to maintain correct gauge*

1 set (4) of double-pointed needles, US Size 4 (3.5mm), *or size needed to maintain correct gauge*

Crochet hook, Size G (4.25mm)

notions

Tapestry needle

Two puffy nylon mesh bath sponges

GAUGE

16 sts and 24 rows = 4 inches square

FINISHED MEASUREMENTS

Washcloth: 14 by 12 inches

directions

JOLLY ROGER WASHCLOTH

note: Design is worked intarsia style: Wind yarn onto bobbins or cut 2-yard lengths of yarn for each section of the picture and background. Follow the chart, reading odd-numbered (RS) rows from right to left, even-numbered (WS) rows from left to right. The background color is black (MC1); the skull and crossbones are white (MC2). The blank squares are knit on RS, purl on WS; dotted squares are purl on RS, knit on WS. A 3-stitch garter-stitch border is maintained on both sides of the flag. Note that the intarsia pattern starts on a WS row. The chart is not symmetrical. With straight needles, cast on 55 stitches in MC1. Work, following chart through Row 72. BO.

crafty tip

Back your knitted washcloth with a piece of terry cloth for extra scrubability.

FINISHING

Weave in yarn ends. Pin piece to measurements and steam on the wrong side.

PARROT

head and body

With green (MC3) and double-pointed needles, CO 30 stitches (10 sts on each of 3 dpns). Join, being careful not to twist, and mark beginning of round. Knit in the round for 7 inches. Begin decreases for head as follows:

Rnd 1: (K8, k2 tog) on each needle 3 times (9 sts per dpn).

Rnd 2: Knit.

Rnd 3: (K7, k2tog) on each needle 3 times (8 sts per dpn).

Rnd 4: Knit

Rnd 5: (K6, k2tog) on each needle 3 times (7 sts per dpn).

Rnd 6: (K5, k2tog) on each needle 3 times (6 sts per dpn).

Rnd 7: (K4, k2tog) on each needle 3 times (5 sts per dpn).

Rnd 8: (K3, k2tog) on each needle 3 times (4 sts per dpn).

Rnd 9: K2tog 6 times (2 sts per dpn).

Cut yarn and thread yarn end through remaining stitches. Draw sts together snugly and fasten off. Weave in yarn tail.

tail feathers

With violet (CC2), CO 9 sts. Work in k1, p1 rib for 2 inches, ending with a WS row. Next row: K1, M1, k7, M1, k1. Continue in St st until piece measures 9 inches. BO.

right wing

With red (CC1) and 2 dpn CO three stitches. Knit in St st for 2½ inches ending on a RS (knit) row. With MC3, knit on 3 new stitches as follows: Pull a MC3 loop knitwise through the last CC1 stitch on the needle, leaving the CC1 stitch on the needle. Put the new MC3 stitch on the left needle (1 new stitch made), pull another loop knitwise through the new MC3 stitch, and put this on the left needle, make 1 more stitch the same way (this cast-on method will give the wing pieces a slight arch). Now knit 3 MC3

stitches and 3 CC1 stitches in St st for 2 more inches, ending on a knit row. Knit on 3 new stitches with CC2 as before. Continue knitting with 3 colors for 1 inch; make 1 more stitch at the CC2 end of the stripe. Continue in St st on 10 stitches (3 CC1, 3 MC3, 4 CC2) until the wing measures 8 inches from the bottom of the CC1 stripe. BO.

left wing

Work to correspond to right wing, adding the new stitches at the end of a purl-side row and then purling them. This will reverse the shaping.

FINISHING

Weave in all ends. Steam press all the completed pieces on the wrong side. Stuff the body of the bird with the nylon mesh sponges (take them apart first

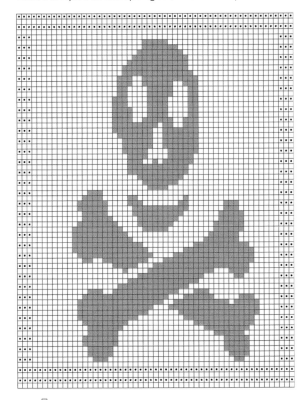

⊡ P ON RS, K ON WS
☐ K ON RS, P ON WS
▨ WHITE
ODD IS RS; WORK CHART LEFT TO RIGHT

by cutting the thread that binds them in the center). Sew the bottom closed with MC3 yarn.

Sew the bound-off edge of the tail feathers to the center of the bird so that the ribbing at the bottom of the tail hangs 2 inches below the bottom of the body. Tack top half of each side of the tail to the body. Position the bound-off edges of the wings so that they are even with the bound-off edge of the tail, overlapping the tail very slightly. Sew the top of the wings in place, tacking the wings to the tail or leaving them free, as you wish.

beak

On dpn, cast on 5 stitches in MC1. Make 3 inches of I-cord (see page 12). Cut yarn and thread yarn end through the stitches, drawing tightly together to finish. Roll the I-cord around itself like a snail and sew rolls in place to maintain the shape, leaving about ½ inch free. Sew securely high on the head of the bird, with the rolled part on the bottom and the free half-inch hooking down.

eyes

With a double strand of MC1 and tapestry needle, make a French knot (see page 16) for each eye.

feet

On dpns, knit 3-stitch I-cord, making 2 strips 2½ inches long and 2 strips 3½ inches long. Sew the two 2-inch strips to the bottom of the parrot with several stitches in the middle, leaving the ends free. Then center the longer strips over the shorter strips and sew to the body of the parrot lengthwise, tacking them to the shorter strips and leaving 1½ inches free. Weave in yarn ends and cut excess close to the body of the bird.

EYE PATCH

With MC1, CO 8 stitches. Knit 1 row. Continuing in garter st throughout, on the second row, add 1 stitch to each end, using the M1 increase. Continue knitting every row until eye patch measures 2 inches. BO until the last loop is left on the needle. Starting with this loop, crochet a 14-inch chain (or the appropriate length to tie around your pirate's head) (see page 17). Pull yarn through and cut yarn. Crochet a second 14-inch chain and sew to the corner of the eye patch that is diagonally opposite to the other chain.

HEAD SCARF

On dpns (or 16-inch circular needle), cast on 80 stitches with MC3. Join. Mark end of round. Knit 6

goonie's treasure: pirate bath set

rounds in St st. Continuing in St st, begin stripe pattern: work 1 rnd MC1, 2 MC3, 2 MC1, 3 MC3, 1 MC2, 2 MC3, 2 MC2. Continue in CC1 until piece measures 5 inches from cast-on edge. Begin decreases as follows:

Rnd 1: (K8, k2tog) 8 times (72 sts).

Rnd 2: (K4, k2 tog) 12 times (60 sts).

Rnd 3: (K3, k2 tog) 12 times (48 sts).

Rnd 4: (K4, k2 tog) 8 times (40 sts).

Rnd 5: (K3, k2 tog) 8 times (32 sts).

Rnd 6: K3, k2 tog, (k6, k2tog) 3 times (28 sts).

Rnd 7: (K5, k2 tog) 4 times (24 sts).

Rnd 8: (K4, k2 tog) 4 times (20 sts).

Rnd 9: (K3, k2 tog) 4 times (16 sts).

Rnd 10: (K2 tog, k2) 4 times (12 sts).

Rnd 11: (K2 tog) 6 times (6 sts).

Cut yarn and thread through remaining 6 stitches. Draw sts together and fasten off.

tie for cap

With CC1, cast on 3 stitches. Row 1: Knit 3. Row 2: K1, M1, k1, M1, k1. Row 3: K5. Next row begin stripes: Knitting every row, work 2 rows MC1, 4 rows CC1, 2 rows MC2. Continue in CC1 for 4 more inches, ending on a WS row, then knit 2 rows MC2, 4 rows CC1, 2 rows MC1, 1 row CC1. Next row: K1, sl 1, k2tog, psso, k1. Next row: Bind off last 3 stitches. (On one end of the tie, the stripes will be on the wrong side, and on the other they'll be on the right side.)

Weave in yarn ends. Steam the cap and the tie on the wrong side. Knot the tie so that the stripes show one end right side, one end wrong side, and sew it to the bottom of the cap, at the back.

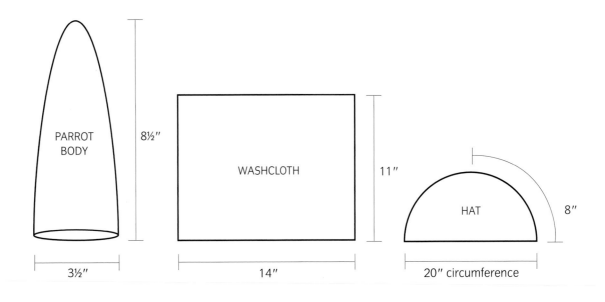

cocoon

nap sack

VICKIE HOWELL • LEVEL: *summer camp*

This nap sack is perfect for a sleepover or nap time. The luxurious cotton chenille, coupled with its handmade goodness, will keep your child feeling cozy whether at home reading a book or away at day care.

yarn

Colinette Fandango (100%
cotton, 100m per 100g hank):

7 hanks of Color Jewel

needles

29-inch circular needle, US Size
13 (9mm), *or size needed to
maintain correct gauge*

Crochet hook, Size N (10mm)

notions

Travel-size pillow

Tapestry needle

GAUGE

9 sts = 4 inches

FINISHED SIZE

54 by 38 inches, excluding pillow

directions

CO 122 sts. Work 6 rows in garter stitch (knit every
row).

Next row (RS): P6, k110, p6.

Next row (WS): K6, p110, k6.

Repeat these last two rows until blanket measures
37 inches, ending with a RS row.

Next row (WS): BO first 82 purlwise; p36, k6, for
pillow (42 sts).

Next row (RS): P6, k36.

Next row (WS): P36, k6.

Repeat these two rows until pillowcase measures
25 inches. BO.

FINISHING

Fold pillowcase in half and seam at the bottom and
left-hand side, being sure to leave right-hand side
(side with border) open so that pillow can be
removed easily for washing nap sack.

Fold blanket section in half lengthwise. Seam
together at bottom and for first 12 inches up the
side.

note: The sleep sack will seem really wide. Keep in
mind, though, that there should be plenty of room
for the child to snuggle up and get comfy.

With crochet hook, half double crochet (see page
18) across top edge (about 97 sts).

Weave in yarn ends.

crafty tip

**For a thriftier, more practical version
of this project, rip a bedsheet into ¼"
strips. Tie strips together, wind into a
ball, and knit as instructed above!**

real genius

memory cards

VICKIE HOWELL • **LEVEL:** *playdate*

This is a knitted version of the classic kid's game. You remember the one. The player lays all of the cards facedown and then turns them over two at a time trying to find a match. If the two cards selected do not match each other, then both cards are turned back over. The object of the game: to find all of the matches.

yarn

Berroco Softwist Bulky (41% wool/59% rayon, 136yd/126m):

1 ball each of Turquoise (MC), Marzipan (CC1), Pitch Black (CC2), Cool Red (CC3), and Nouveau Berry (CC4)

needles

1 pair of straight needles US Size 8 (5mm), or size needed to maintain correct gauge

notions

½ yard cotton fabric

Sewing needle and thread

Tapestry needle

GAUGE

18 sts and 24 rows = 4 inches

FINISHED MEASUREMENT

5 by 4¾ inches

directions

With Turquoise (MC), CO 22 sts. Working in St st with a reverse stockinette stitch border, follow the charts for each card. Make 2 of each.

FINISHING

Weave in yarn ends.

Cut fabric into 4½- by 4½-inch squares. Press ¼ inch under each edge to create hem. Pin fabric square to back of memory card and sew on with needle and thread.

mama tip

This is a great game to occupy your child on plane trips. It won't take up much room in your bag and is easily played on a tray table!

chart key

Blank square = K on RS, P on WS

"o" = P on RS, K on WS.

"X" = duplicate stitch in MC

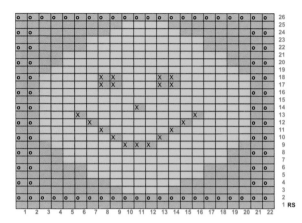

happy face

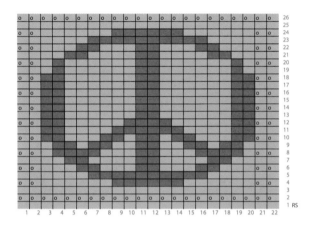

peace sign

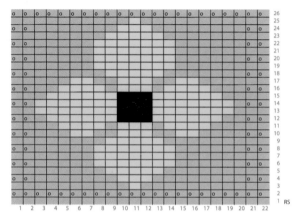

flower

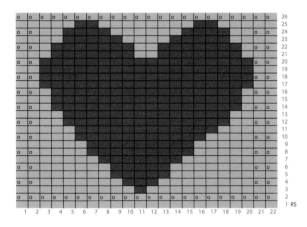

heart

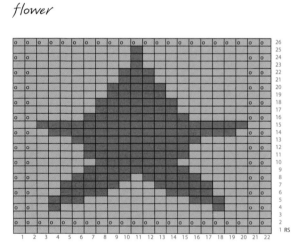

star

dance tv

striped leg warmers & bag

KERRIE RYCROFT • **LEVEL:** *playdate*

When the opportunity to design something that a child would really want, who better to turn to than your three-year-old daughter who has an opinion on everything, especially her mother's knitting. "Um," she replied. "I'd really like you to knit me something that is beautiful colors, stripy and comes with its own special bag." We talked about gloves, scarves, slippers, and sweaters before I suggested leg warmers. "Legwarmers, what are they?" she asked.

yarn

Rowan All Seasons Cotton (60% Cotton, 40% Acrylic; 90m per 50g ball):

For legwarmers (all sizes): 1 ball Color 183 Jaunty (red)

1 ball Color 202 Soul (pink)

1 ball Color 18 Jazz (blue)

1 ball Color 178 Organic (white)

For carrying bag: 2 balls Color 202 Soul (pink)

1 ball Color 183 Jaunty (red)

1 ball Color 178 Organic (white)

needles

1 pair of straight needles US Size 8 (5mm), *or size needed to maintain correct gauge*

24-inch circular needle US Size 8 (5mm), or size needed to maintain correct gauge

notions

Stitch markers

About 3 feet of white cord or ribbon for fastening bag

About 3 feet 1½-inch (38mm) wide cotton webbing in white for bag handles

Tapestry needle

~~~~~~

Not a child of the eighties, she had no idea what I was talking about. I tried to explain what they were but was met with a blank stare. It seemed easiest just to make one to show her. When I held up a finished leg warmer for her approval, she smiled and said, "Oh, it's like a sweater sleeve for your leg—only without the rest of the sweater." Why didn't I think of explaining it that way? Why the matching bag? Honestly, I have no idea. I just know that she loves anything that comes with its own box or bag that it can be safely stored away in at night. These leg warmers are no exception they are easy enough for the most impatient young child to be able to put on and take off herself and can be carried around in the bag when not being worn. The All Seasons Cotton is soft and light to wear and looks fab in any bright color combination. Have fun experimenting with different colors, lengths, and stripe combinations to make your child a truly individual pair of "sweater sleeves without the rest of the sweater!"

GAUGE

4½ sts by 6 rows = 4 inches

LEG WARMER SIZES

3–4 (5–6, 7–8) years

directions

LEG WARMERS

stripe sequence

For all sizes, start with:

3 rows pink, increasing on middle row

2 rows blue

1 row white

3 rows red, increasing on middle row

2 rows pink

2 rows white

1 row pink

3 rows blue, increasing on middle row

2 rows white

For small size (3 to 4 years) only: End sequence with 2 rows red

Repeat entire sequence for small size once more.

For medium size (5 to 6 years) only: End sequence with:

1 row pink

3 rows red, increasing on middle row

1 row blue

Repeat entire sequence for medium size once more.

For large size (7 to 8 years) only: End sequence with:

2 rows red

1 row pink

2 rows blue

1 row white

3 rows red, increasing on middle row

Repeat entire sequence for large size once more.

Using straight needles and red cast on 34 (38, 42) stitches. Work 6 rows in k1, p1 rib.

K1 row.

Beginning with a purl row, work in St st, working the stripe sequence for the relevant size, increasing 1 stitch at each end of the row on the middle row where 3 rows are worked. This will ensure that the increase is not obvious when you change color.

Where possible, carry the yarns up the side of the work. If cutting yarn, leave a yarn end about 4 inches long to sew seam when the leg warmer is completed.

Change to pink and work one row in St st. Work 6 rows in k1, p1 rib. Bind off in rib.

FINISHING
Matching colors, use any loose yarn ends to seam the leg warmer. Weave in all remaining ends. Block following the instructions on the yarn label.

BAG
Starting with bottom, using straight needles and red, CO 40 stitches and work 22 rows in seed (or moss) stitch, working as follows: * K1, p1; rep from * across. Row 2: * P1, k1; rep from * across. Rep these 2 rows 11 times. BO.

For sides of bag, using pink and circular needle, pick up 40 stitches along cast-on edge, pm, pick up 22 stitches from short side, pm, pick up 40 stitches from bound-off edge, pm, and pick up 22 stitches from other short side, pm (124 sts).

Knitting each rnd, work 54 rounds and dec 1 st before each marker on every 10th rnd 5 times (104 sts).

Eyelet rnd: * K2, yo, k2tog; repeat from * around.

K 4 rnds.

Picot eyelet rnd: K1, * yo, k2tog; repeat from * around.

Switch to red yarn and knit 2 rnds for top hem. Bind off loosely.

Fold hem at picot eyelet rnd to the inside of bag. A picot edging forms at the top of the bag. Stitch hem in place, taking care that the first eyelet row is not covered by the hem.

HANDLES

note: I originally used moss stitch handles for the bag made in red and I-cord as a fastening. After I gave the first version of the bag to my daughter, she spun it around on the handles so much that the handles stretched out of shape quickly. Then I decided to go with the more secure webbing straps and a matching cord fastening. I have included details for moss stitch handles and I-cord fastening.

option 1: Cut 2 lengths of cotton webbing to the desired length and sew to the top and bottom of side of the bag.

option 2: Using straight needles and red, cast on 8 stitches and work in seed (or moss) stitch until straps are desired length. Make 2nd strap in the same way. Attach to top and bottom of side of the bag as above. If desired, back knitted straps with cotton webbing straps, sewing edges together.

DRAWSTRING

option 1: Cut a yard (or meter) length of cotton cord and thread through the eyelets, starting in the center front. Tie as required.

option 2: Using straight needles and white CO 3 stitches and work a 3-stitch I-cord to about 1 yard (or meter) in length. Thread through eyelets as above.

FINISHING

Weave in yarn ends and block.

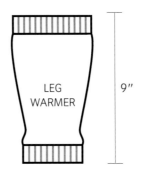
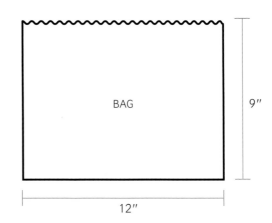

dance tv: striped leg warmers & bag

purls just wanna have fun
twirly tank

JILLIAN MORENO FOR ACME KNITTING COMPANY • LEVEL: *playdate*

Equal parts ballerina, fairy & whirling dervish, this tank is perfect for the girls of per-
petual motion. With button on & off fringe your twirling girly can change her look as
easily as she changes her mind, plus being a quickie knit means that in a couple of
nights your girl can be ready to twist and shout.

MATERIALS

yarn

Crystal Palace Cotton Chenille (100% cotton, 98 yd per 50g skein):

2 (2, 2) skeins Color 9660, purple (MC)

For Fringes: Crystal Palace Splash (100% polyester; 94 yd per 100g ball):

1 skein Color 7234, Pink & Purple Mix (CC1) AND

Crystal Palace Squiggle (50% nylon, 50% polyester, 100 yd per 50g skein):

1 skein Color 9289, Variegated

Purple & Green (CC2) AND

Crystal Palace Fizz (100% polyester, 120 yd per 50g skein):

1 skein Color 9404, Rainbow (CC3) AND

Crystal Palace Choo Choo (52% rayon, 30% polyester, 18% nylon, 92 yd per 50g skein):

1 skein Color 1710, Green (CC4)

needles

1 set(s) US #5 (3.5mm) straight needles or circulars, any length, *or size needed to maintain correct gauge*

Crochet hook Size K

notions

10 backing buttons, ¾-inch diameter

10 decorative 1-inch buttons

Sewing needle

Sewing thread to match chenille yarn

Tapestry needle

GAUGE

16 sts and 20 rows = 4 inches in stockinette stitch

SIZE

2 (4, 6) years

FINISHED MEASUREMENTS

Chest: 23 (25, 28) inches

Length: 8½ (9½, 10½) inches

crafty tip

For a little extra razzle-dazzle, use strands of beads or sequins in place of the hanging yarn bits.

directions

BACK

With straight needles, CO 46 (50, 56) sts, K 2 rows.

P 1 row, k 1 row, p 1 row.

Buttonhole rows:

Row 1: Continuing in St st, k6 (8, 11), *BO 2, k6; rep from * 3 times, BO 2, k6 (8, 11) (5 buttonholes made).

Row 2: P6 (8, 11), *CO 2, p6; rep from * 3 times, CO 2, p6 (8, 11).

Work in St st until piece measures 3½ (4, 4) inches.

Armhole: BO 3 (4, 5) sts at beg of next 2 rows [40 (42, 46) sts].

Continue in St st until piece measures 4½ (5½, 5½) inches.

Back Neck: Work 9 (9, 10) sts; attach second ball of yarn, with new yarn BO center 22 (24, 26) sts, work to end. Work each side with its separate yarn and dec 1 st at each neck edge, on next row [8 (8, 9) sts on each side].

Work even on each side in St st until back measures 8¼ (9¼, 10¼) inches. BO all stitches.

FRONT

Work same as for back to back neck shaping [40 (42, 46) sts].

Front Neck: Work 13 (13, 15) sts; attach second ball of yarn; with new yarn BO center 14 (16, 16) sts; work to end.

Working each side with its own yarn, dec 1 st at neck edge every other row 5 (5, 6) times [8 (8, 9) sts on each side].

Work in St st until back measures 8¼ (9¼, 10¼) inches. BO all stitches.

FINISHING

Sew side and shoulder seams.

Using crochet hook and a strand each of green (CC4) and rainbow (CC3) held together, work single crochet (see page 17) around armhole and neck edges. Steam block tank.

BUTTONS

Cut ten 24-inch lengths of each fringe yarn.

Arrange yarns into 10 groups, each group containing 1 strand of each different yarn. Knot each group loosely in the center. Sandwich knot between decorative button and backing button and sew buttons together through loose yarn knot. Button the backing button to tank with the decorative buttons and yarn fringes on the right side of the tank. Twirl away!

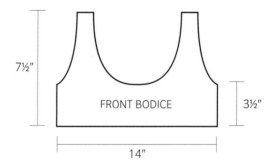

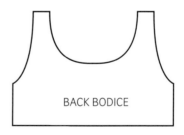

measurements same,
only difference is neck size

greatest american hero
super kid cape

VICKIE HOWELL • LEVEL: *weekend at nana's*

In the land of pint-sized superheroes, the right attire is essential for crime fighting success. This vibrant, cotton cape will keep your favorite little protector both cool and collected under the pressures of battling the bad guys. Knit it up as shown, or make a wool version to keep your caped crusader warm on even the chilliest of adventures!

MATERIALS

yarn

Araucania Nature Cotton (100% cotton, 165 yd per ball):

4 (5) balls red (MC)

1 ball gold (CC)

needles

29-inch circular needle, US Size 6 (4.25mm), *or size needed to maintain correct gauge*

notion

Tapestry needle

~~~~~~

GAUGE

16 sts and 24 rows = 4 inches

SIZE

Child's 2–4 (6–8) years

directions

Starting at neck with red, CO 32 (36) sts. Knit 5 rows.

Row 6: *Inc 1 in next st, k3; repeat from * to end [40 (45) sts].

Row 7: Purl.

Row 8 (eyelet row for tie): K1 (2), *yo, k2tog; repeat from * to last st, k1.

Row 9: Purl.

Increase section: Next row (RS): K1 (3), *inc 1 in next st, k1, inc 1 in next st; repeat from * [66 (73) sts]. P 1 row, k 1 row, p 1 row.

Next inc row (RS): K2 (4), *inc 1 in next st, k1; repeat from *, ending k2 (5) [97 (105) sts]. P 1 row, k 1 row, p 1 row.

Next inc row (RS): K3 (5), *inc 1 in next st, k2; repeat from *, ending k4 (7) [127 (136) sts]. P 1 row, k 1 row, p 1 row.

Next inc row (RS): K4 (6), *inc 1 in next st, k3; repeat to last 3 (10) sts; inc in next st, k2 (9) [158 (167) sts].

Continuing in St st, inc 3 sts (1 at each end and 1 in middle of row) every other row twice (once) [164 (170) sts].

Knit even in St st. When piece measures 5 inches, begin lightening bolt chart as follows:

Next row (RS): Knit 67 (70) sts k30 sts. of chart, reading chart right to left on RS rows, k67 (70) sts.

Next row (WS): Purl 67 (70) sts, p30 sts of chart, reading chart left to right on WS rows, p67 (70) sts.

crafty tip

As an alternative to working the lighting-bolt pattern in intarsia, knit the cape without the design and then just sew on a fabric or felt version of the image after you've finished!

Continue in this manner until chart is completed. Continue to work even until cape measures 17 (19) inches from beg.

Knit 5 rows (garter stitch) in gold. BO.

FINISHING
Weave in yarn ends. Block.

MAKE TIE
Knit 24-inch I-cord tie (see page 12) in gold or cut length of ribbon or seam binding.

Lace tie through eyelet row, and voilà, your little superhero is ready to go off and save the world!

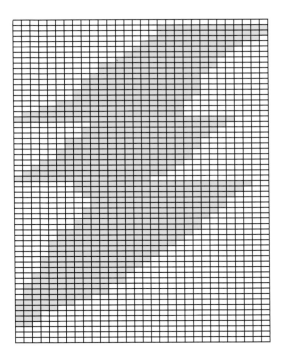

For younger children, I recommend sewing some Velcro to a fabric or grosgrain ribbon tab instead of using a tie. This will ensure that the cape doesn't become a choking hazard.

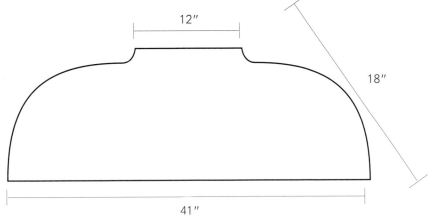

12"

18"

41"

greatest american hero: super kid cape

the last unicorn
unicorn dress-up

CHRISTINA BENEDETTI • **LEVEL:** *weekend at nana's*

I've always loved making and wearing costumes, and like many young girls, I loved unicorns as a child. This pattern is just the latest in a long line of drawings of unicorns, stories about unicorns, and hours spent pretending I was a unicorn when I was younger. I picked the brightest colors I could find for the sample, but it would look great in pastels or darker tones, depending on your child's preferences. Try using two colors on the horn! Go wild! And since the tail and embellishments don't use too much yarn, mixing and matching from your scrap-yarn stash could be an option too.

yarn

Cascade 220 (100% wool, 220 yd per 100g skein):

1 skein Color 7826, orange (MC1)

1 skein Color 7828, yellow (CC) AND

Crystal Palace Splash (100% polyester, 94 yd per 100g skein):

1 skein Color 9480, multicolor fuzzy yarn (MC2)

needles

1 pair each straight needles, US size 13 (9mm), US size 11 (8mm), and US size 10 (6.5mm), *or size needed to maintain correct gauge*

1 set (4) double-pointed needles (dpn) US Size 11 (8mm), *or size needed to maintain correct gauge*

notions

2 to 3 feet of nylon strap for belt

Belt buckle

2 feet ¼-inch wide elastic

Sewing needle

Threads to match yarns

Tapestry needle

GAUGE

14 sts and 24 rows = 4 inches in garter st with single strand of wool yarn on medium-sized straight needles.

12 sts and 16 rows = 4 inches in St st with double strand of wool yarn on medium-sized straight needles.

directions

HEADPIECE

horn (make 2)

With 2 strands of yellow (CC) held together (double stranded), using double-pointed needles, CO 12 sts onto one of the needles. Divide evenly among 3 needles. Join in the (very small) round.

Knit in St st for 1½ inches. On the next round, k4, k2tog, k4, k2tog (10 sts). Continue in St st for 1 inch more (2½ inches from beg). On the next round, k3, k2tog, k3, k2tog (8 sts).

Continue for 1 inch more (3½ inches from beg). On the next round, k2, k2tog, k2, k2tog (6 sts).

After this point, begin working in I-cord (see page 12) fashion on 2 dpn. Continue for 1 inch more (4½ inches from beg). On the next row, k1, k2tog, k1, k2tog (4 sts).

Continue for 1 inch more (5½ inches from beg). On the next row, k2tog twice (2 sts).

Continue for 1 inch more (6½ inches from beg). On next row, k2tog (1 st). K this stitch again; cut yarn, then pull yarn end through the loop to bind off. Weave in yarn ends.

ear (make 2)

With orange (MC1) double-stranded and dpns, CO 8 sts. K 1 row. P 1 row.

Row 3: K1, inc 1 in next st (by knitting into front and back of loop), k to last 2 sts, inc 1 in next st, k1 (10 sts)

Row 4: Purl.

Work 4 rows in St st.

Row 9: K1, k2tog 4 times, K1 (6 sts).

Row 10: P1, p2tog twice, p1 (4 sts).

Row 11: Knit.

BO in purl. Weave in yarn ends.

HORN BASE
With orange (MC1) double-stranded and medium-sized needles, CO 18 sts. Work 5 rows in garter st (knit every row) and BO. Weave in yarn ends. Set this piece aside.

HEADPIECE
With orange (MC1) single-stranded and medium-sized needles, CO 35 sts.

Row 1: Knit.

Row 2: K1, inc 1, k to end.

Row 3: Knit.

Repeat these three rows 4 times more (40 sts).

Row 16: Knit.

Row 17: K1, dec 1, k to end.

Row 18 Knit.

Repeat these three rows 4 times more (35 sts). BO. Weave in yarn ends. Set this piece aside.

FURRY EMBELLISHMENT
This piece will be sewn around the horn base, hiding it.

With fuzzy yarn (MC2) and small needles, CO 16 sts. K6 rows in garter st. BO. Weave in yarn ends. Set this piece aside.

Now it's time to hand felt! (See page 14)

I found that my final product looked better if I felted all my little pieces separately, then sewed them together at the end. The pieces will felt more evenly, and you'll have more control over the final placement of the ears and horn.

FINISHING

horn
When the two felted horn pieces are still damp, twist them around each other and secure them as you want them to look. I used black metal office binder clips to hold them together, but you could also pin the twisted pieces to an ironing board.

Once the pieces have dried, thread a large sewing needle with thread to match the yarn and insert it at the top of the horn. Pass it down through the center of the horn, catching the twists as you go. Your needle won't be long enough to go all the way down, so push it down as far as it will go, pull it tight, and continue down the center of the horn. Secure the thread. Stitch the two pieces together more carefully at the top and bottom of the horn.

headpiece
Fold each ear in half lengthwise; because they were worked in stockinette st, they should naturally curl in on the purl side. Stitch each top together with matching thread. Fold the horn base lengthwise into a cylinder and stitch it together.

note: When stitching the horn base and ears onto the headpiece, make a few basting stitches to hold each unit in place, then stitch them on properly.

Mark the center of the headpiece and position the horn base accordingly. Stitch the horn base in place. Measure approximately one inch from the horn base in each direction, and position the ears. Stitch them in place.

Insert the horn into the horn base and stitch the two together around the upper edge of the horn base. Place the furry embellishment over the horn base and stitch it in place.

Try the completed headpiece on your child and cut the elastic to fit his or her head. Sew ends of the elastic chin strap to the underside of the headpiece.

TAIL
The tail is created using a loop stitch on the right side, and purling on the wrong side. The loop stitch makes it fluffy; working in stockinette st makes the tail curl in.

knitted loop stitch pattern
K 1 row.

Loop row (RS): K1, *k1 and leave original on left needle, bring yarn to front of work under tip of needle, wyif loop over left thumb (extend thumb to lengthen loop); keeping loop on thumb, return yarn to back of work under tip of needle, wyib k same st again and drop original st from left needle; pass first st over second as if to bind off; rep from * to last st, k1.

Next row (WS): Purl.

Repeat last 2 rows for pattern.

With fuzzy yarn (MC2) and largest straight needles, CO 12 sts. Work in loop stitch pattern for 22 rows. Work in garter st. BO.

FINISHING
Sew the garter-stitch flap down around the nylon belt strap. Try the tail/belt on your child. Attach the belt buckle and trim the nylon strap to fit.

WRISTBANDS (MAKE 2)
These simple wristbands will add the finishing touch to your little unicorn!

Using fuzzy yarn (MC2) and smallest needles, CO 16 sts. Work in k2, p2 rib for 5 rows. BO in rib. Stitch the sides to form wristband. Weave in yarn ends.

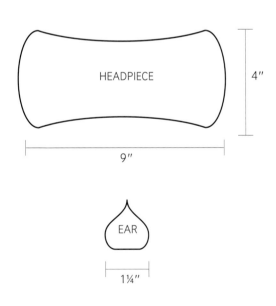

HEADPIECE

4"

9"

EAR

1¼"

blanche devereux
furry stole & fancy purse

VICKIE HOWELL • **LEVEL:** *playdate*

Every girl, no matter what her age, needs something furry and sparkly to add a little glamour to her life. Knit these pieces up for the little diva in your life and maybe she'll even let you borrow them for your own night out on the town.

MATERIALS

yarn

Crystal Palace Splash (100% polyester, 94 yd per 100g ball):

1 ball Color Italian Ice (MC) AND

Crystal Palace Shimmer (100% Polyester, 94 yd per 100g ball):

1 ball Color Strawberry (CC)

needles

1 pair straight needles, US Size 11 (8mm), *or size needed to maintain correct gauge*

Crochet hook, Size H (5mm)

notions

Tapestry needle

½ yard satin fabric for purse lining

Sewing thread in coordinating color

Sewing needle

Vintage button

Sewing machine (optional)

~~~~~~

GAUGE

5 sts = 1 inch in garter st

FINISHED MEASUREMENTS

Stole: 38 ½ (including crocheted border) by 3 inches

Purse: 6 ½ by 4 inches

directions

FURRY STOLE

With Italian Ice (MC), CO 15 sts. Work in garter stitch until piece measures 36½ inches. BO.

With Strawberry (CC) and crochet hook, crochet one row of single crochet across end of stole (see page 17) 15 sts. Crochet chain 3, turn.

Next row: 2 double crochet in first sc (see page 18), *sl st in next sc, 3 double crochet in next sc; repeat from * to end. Tie off. Repeat on opposite end. Weave in yarn ends.

SPARKLY PURSE

With Strawberry (CC), CO 25 sts. Work in seed stitch as follows: K1, repeat (p1, k1) to end on every row. Work even in seed st for 8 inches

Shape front flap as follows: Next RS (decrease) row: Ssk; keeping pattern as established, work to last 2 sts, k2tog.

Repeat decrease row every other row twice.

Repeat decrease row every row 4 times (11 sts).

Buttonhole row: Ssk, work 2 sts in seed st, yo, k2tog (buttonhole made), work 2 sts in seed st, k2tog.

Work 2 rows in seed st.

Repeat decrease row twice. BO remaining sts in seed st.

FINISHING

Fold bottom 4 inches of bag up with WS together. Seam sides of bag. Cut out 8½ by 13-inch piece of satin. Fold fabric in half with RS together and machine (or hand) sew sides, making ¼-inch seams. Insert lining into purse; fold under ¼ inch at top edge and sew to inside of bag with sewing thread (flap is unlined).

Sew on button to correspond to flap buttonhole.

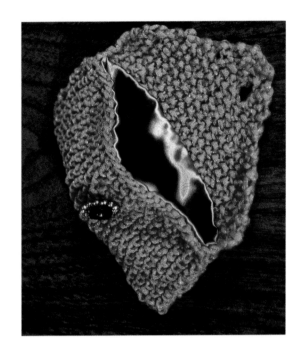

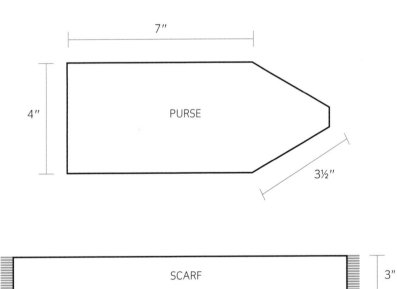

princess buttercup
fancy dress

CANDI JENSEN • **LEVEL:** *weekend at nana's*

I'm lucky enough to live in a neighborhood filled with wonderful young children. They are young enough not to care what people think and use their imaginations to the fullest (you remember how that was). Two little girls in particular, Samantha and Claire, are just a blast to watch as they run up and down the street in their princess dresses. They may be carrying a sword to do battle with the boys or climbing a tree, but they always have on their sparkly dresses and shoes. It's just so much fun to think of how free-spirited they are and how much fun they have without feeling they have to adhere to any particular sense of decorum. They are truly an inspiration.

MATERIALS

yarn

Patons Brilliant (69% acrylic, 19% nylon, 12% polyester, 166 yd/151m per 50g ball):

1 (2, 2) balls Color 3425, pink (MC)

1 (1, 1) ball Color 3023, gold (CC)

needles

1 pair each of straight needles, US Size 10 (6mm), *or size to maintain correct gauge,* and US Size 8 (5mm)

Crochet hook, Size F (3.75mm)

notions

Yarn needle

1 yard pink lightweight satin (at least 54 inches wide) for skirt

1 yard gold shimmer fabric (at least 54 inches wide) for skirt

Sewing needle

Sewing thread to match fabrics

Tapestry needle

GAUGE

16 sts and 20 rows = 4 inches in St st on larger needles, with 2 strands held together

SIZES

2 (4, 6) years

FINISHED MEASUREMENTS

Chest: 22 (24, 26) inches

OPEN STITCH PATTERN

Row 1: K1, *k2 tog, yo; repeat from *, ending k1.

Row 2 and 4: P, making sure to purl the yo sts

Row 3: K1, *yo, k2 tog; repeat from *, ending k1.

Repeat these 4 rows for pattern.

directions

BACK

With pink (MC) and 2 strands of yarn held together, using larger needles, cast on 44 (48, 52) sts and work in St st for 2 (2½, 3) inches, ending with a p row.

ARMHOLE

Bind off 4 sts at the beg of the next 2 rows [36 (40, 44) sts]. Continue until piece measures 3½ (4, 5) inches. Work across 18 (20, 22) sts, turn. Working on just these sts, work until strap measures 5 (5½, 5½) inches. Bind off. Join yarn to other side and work until piece is the same length.

crafty tip

As an alternative to making a new skirt for this project, recycle one of your child's dresses by cutting off the old fabric bodice and sewing the skirt portion onto the new fabulous knitted one!

FRONT

Work as for back until piece measures 3½ (4, 5) inches, ending with a p row. Work across 15 (17, 19) sts, bind off the center 6 sts for front neck, k remaining 15 (17, 19) sts for right front. Working on right front sts only, p 1 row. Bind off 2 (3, 3) at neck edge, then 2 sts at neck edge every other row once, then 1 (2, 2) sts once. Work even on 10 (11, 12) sts until piece is the same length as back to shoulder. BO all sts. Join yarn to neck edge of left side. Starting with a p row, shape neck to correspond to right front, reversing shaping by binding off at beg of purl rows.

SLEEVE

With CC and 1 strand of yarn, using smaller needles cast on 33 (39, 43) sts; purl 1 row (wrong side). Begin open stitch and work until piece measures 4 (5, 5) inches; bind off. Make 2.

FINISHING

Sew side and shoulder seams of bodice. Sew top of sleeves to armholes; sew underarm seams. With smaller needles, pick up 6 sts for the bind off, then 4 sts for every 5 rows, then repeat for other side around neck. Knit 1 row, then work 2 rows of open stitch. Bind off. Sew button at top of left back opening. With a crochet hook, chain a button loop (sse page 17). Sew ends of loop in place on right back opposite the button.

SKIRT

From each fabric, cut 2 pieces each 15 (16, 18) inches long by 22 (23, 24) inches wide. With right sides of satin pieces together and using ½-inch seam allowance, sew side seams. Repeat with shimmer fabric. With shimmer fabric as outer layer, hold both fabrics together and gather one long edge of skirt; adjust gathers to fit bottom edge of bodice. Sew in place. Hem the skirt to the desired length. I suggest about a 2-inch hem.

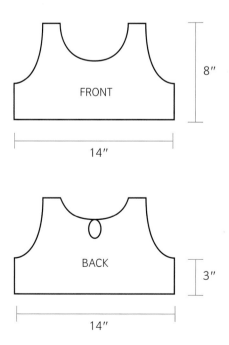

princess buttercup: fancy dress

benetar
guitar pillow

VICKIE HOWELL · **LEVEL:** *weekend at nana's*

I've always been a closet rock star. I do not play an instrument or sing, but, man, I love to pretend that I do! This project was born out of the hope that I can instill the power of music and creative expression into my own children.

yarn

Lamb's Pride Worsted (85% wool, 15% mohair 190 yd/173m per skein):

For guitar: 1 skein Color Lotus Pink (MC)

Small amount of Color Crème (CC)

For pick: Small amount of any color

needles

1 pair of straight needles, US Size 8 (5mm), *or size needed to maintain correct gauge*

Crochet hook, Size H (5mm)

notions

Tapestry needle

Polyester fiberfill

~~~~~~

GAUGE
18 sts = 4 inches

FINISHED MEASUREMENTS
Guitar: 11 by 33 inches

Pick: About 3 by 3¼ inches (felted)

directions

GUITAR
BACK
With Lotus Pink (MC), CO 12 sts. Work 2 rows in St st.

Next row (RS): Increasing 1 st at beg and end of row, knit across. P 1 row. Repeat these 2 rows until you have 44 sts. Work even in St st for 6 rows.

Next RS row: Ssk, k to last 2 sts, k2tog. P 1 row. Repeat these 2 rows until you have 24 sts.

Next RS row: Increasing 1 st at beg and end of row, knit across. P 1 row. Repeat these 2 rows until you have 36 sts. Work even in St st for 6 rows.

Next RS row: Ssk, k to last 2 sts, k2tog. P 1 row. Repeat these 2 rows until you have 24 sts.

Next RS row: BO 7 sts, k10, BO last 7 sts. Cut yarn.

NECK
(WS) Attach Crème (CC); work in St st until neck measures 13 inches.

RS row: Ssk, k to end. P 1 row. Repeat these 2 rows until 2 sts remain. BO.

crafty tip

To give this project some additional play-ability, along with the stuffing add a piece of cardboard that's been cut into the shape of the guitar.

FRONT

With MC, CO 12 sts. Work 2 rows in St st.

Next row (RS): Increasing 1 st (at each end), knit across. P 1 row. Repeat these 2 rows until you have 44 sts. Work even St st for 3 rows.

RS: With MC, k17, switch to CC and k10, switch to MC, k to end.

WS: With MC, p17, switch to CC and p10, switch to MC, p to end.

Repeat last 2 rows once more (this will create the mock guitar bridge).

On the last row, start decreasing (at the same time) as follows:

Ssk, k to last 2 sts, k2 tog. P 1 row. Repeat these 2 rows until you have 30 sts.

Next RS row: Ssk, k9; join and k9 in CC; attach another small bal of MC and k to last 2 with MC, k2 tog.

Next row: P10 in MC, p9 in CC, p10 in MC (this sequence created your first mock "pick-up").

With MC only, continue dec as before at beginning and end of every k row until you have 24 sts.

Next RS row: K1, M1, k to last st, M1, k1. Continue to inc every k row 3 times.

Next RS row: K1, M1, k11, join CC and k9, k10, M1, k1 in MC.

Next row (WS): P12 in MC, p9 in CC, p to end in MC (second mock pick-up created).

With MC only, continue inc until you have 36 sts.

Work 7 rows even in St st.

Next RS row: Dec as before at each end of every k row until you have 32 sts. Continue to dec and at

the same time knit in third pick-up in same manner as used for the first 2. Continue to dec until you have 24 sts.

Next RS Row: BO 7 sts, k10, BO last 7 sts. Cut yarn.

Neck: Same as for back until 2 sts remain. BO.

FINISHING

Using satin stitch (see photo) and CC, embroider a saying (for example, Rock'n' Roll, Folk, Jazz, I Rock!, etc.) or your little rock star's name on the front of the guitar.

Using French knot stitch (see page 16) and MC, embroider 6 tuning pegs onto the top side of the neck.

With RS facing, sew front and back together using preferred method. I generally use the single crochet method (see page 17) worked on the RS for this type of item. It creates a nice, even, durable seam. Make sure you leave at least a 3-inch opening at the base of the neck. Turn so right sides are out. Stuff guitar; sew up opening.

FELTED PICK (MAKE 2)

CO 4 sts. K 1 row. P 1 row.

Row 3 (RS): K1, M1, k to last st, M1, k1 (6 sts).

P 1 row, k 1 row, p 1 row.

Repeat last 4 rows once (8 sts).

RS row: Repeat Row 3 (10 sts).

Next row: Purl.

BO all sts.

FINISHING

With right sides together, sew 2 sides of the pick together. Turn right side out and sew last side. Felt pick by hand (see page 14).

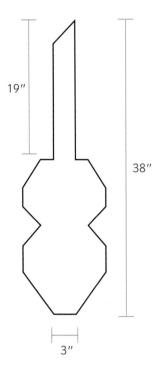

19″

38″

3″

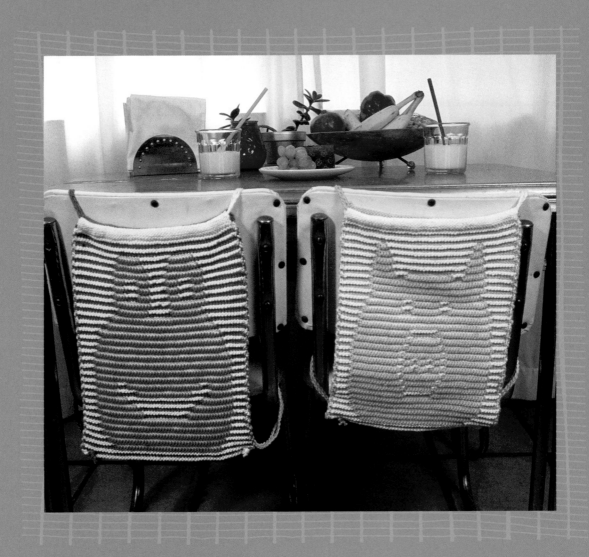

carry-all chameleon

illusion backpacks

SHETHA NOLKE • LEVEL: *weekend at nana's*

These satchels are handy as backpacks or shoulder bags and they come with a built-in friend. The finished bag measures about 10½ by 13½ inches, which is perfect for carrying all the essentials.

MATERIALS

yarn

Plymouth Fantasy Naturale (100% mercerized cotton, 140 yd per skein):

For Froggy: 2 skeins Color 8001, white (MC)

2 skeins Color 5228, green (CC1)

For Piggy: 2 skeins Color 8001, white (MC)

2 skeins Color 6188, pink (CC2)

needles

1 pair straight needles, US Size 7 (4.5 mm), or size needed to maintain correct gauge

Crochet hook, Size G (4.25mm)

Tapestry needle

~~~~~~

The illusion, or shadow, technique involves creating a two-color image using the texture of the knitting. Garter stitch will stand up and stockinette stitch will lie flat. Placing the raised areas in the appropriate places creates the final image. Wherever the foreground image is raised, the background will lie flat, and vice versa. For this project the pattern is in the form of a chart.

crafty tip

As you work, it is important to be sure that your gauge is correct or else the satchel may grow to be quite large and the illusion may not show as well. By working with a smaller needle than the yarn recommends, the fabric is tightly knit and the raised sections are more pronounced.

GAUGE

22 sts and 38 rows creates a 4-inch square in 2 rows stockinette/2 rows garter stitch pattern.

SIZE

One size fits most; the length of the straps will determine fit.

KNITTING TECHNIQUE

The illusion technique requires changing from MC to CC every two rows. Odd-numbered rows are always knit across all stitches. Even-numbered rows are purled for the clear boxes on the chart and knitted for the colored boxes. One set of 2 rows in MC and 2 rows in CC creates one slice of the image. Because only 2 rows are knitted before you go back to the other color, the working yarn can just be carried up the side of the work. This eliminates having to weave in many ends. Note that these charts are symmetrical. This means the charts can be read either from right to left or from left to right, whichever direction is more comfortable for you.

directions

FRONT

Starting at top of bag, cast on 57 stitches in MC. Knit 9 rows in stockinette stitch, knitting on the RS and purling on the WS.

Begin working chart from row 1 (at the bottom). Note: The chart is worked with design upside down. You are working from the top of the bag down to the bottom. The first two rows of the chart are in the MC and the second two are in the CC. This repeats throughout the chart. Note that the first and last stitch of each row are worked in stockinette st. This makes a consistent edge that is easier to sew during finishing.

On row 121 of the chart, create the hole for the shoulder straps: K3, k2tog, yo, k to the last 5 sts, yo, k2tog, to the end.

On row 122, p first stitch, k across to last st, purl last st. Do not bind off.

BACK

After the chart knitting is complete, it's time to knit up the back of the satchel. The back will be worked much like the front, but without the design. The first four rows will have holes to put the straps through later. Work as follows:

First 4 rows:

Row 1: Continuing on sts of row 122, k across all 57 sts in MC.

Row 2: across all sts in MC.

Row 3: With CC, k3, k2tog, yo, k to last 5 sts, yo, k2tog, and k3.

Row 4: P first stitch, k across to last st, p last st.

Pattern for back of bag:

Row 1: K all sts in MC.

Row 2: P all sts in MC.

Row 3: K all sts in CC.

Row 4: P1, k55, p1 in CC.

Repeat this pattern 30 times. There will be a total of 124 rows for the back of the bag (first 4 rows + 120 more). Continuing in CC, work 9 rows in St st; BO all sts.

FINISHING

Sew the cast-on row to the first chart-row to form a tube from the MC St st section. On the back, sew the bind-off row to the last row of the final 4-row pattern. Then sew the side seams of the bag, aligning the top drawstring tubes (leave tubes open) and the holes at the bottom of the bag. Weave in yarn ends.

STRAPS

Make 2, one each in MC and CC as follows: Using crochet hook, chain a string that will be long enough to go up the side of the bag twice and through each of the top tubes (at least 48 inches long), adding several inches for tying a knot. With the pattern side facing, thread one end of one strap into the front tube from the left side, and the other end of the same strap into the back tube, also from the left. Adjust the strap so that the ends are even. Do the same for the other strap, starting from the right side. Pull the two ends of the right-hand strap through the right-side holes at the bottom of the bag. Tie a knot to secure the strap at the base of the bag. Repeat for the left-hand strap. When the straps are pulled, the top tubes of the bag should draw in.

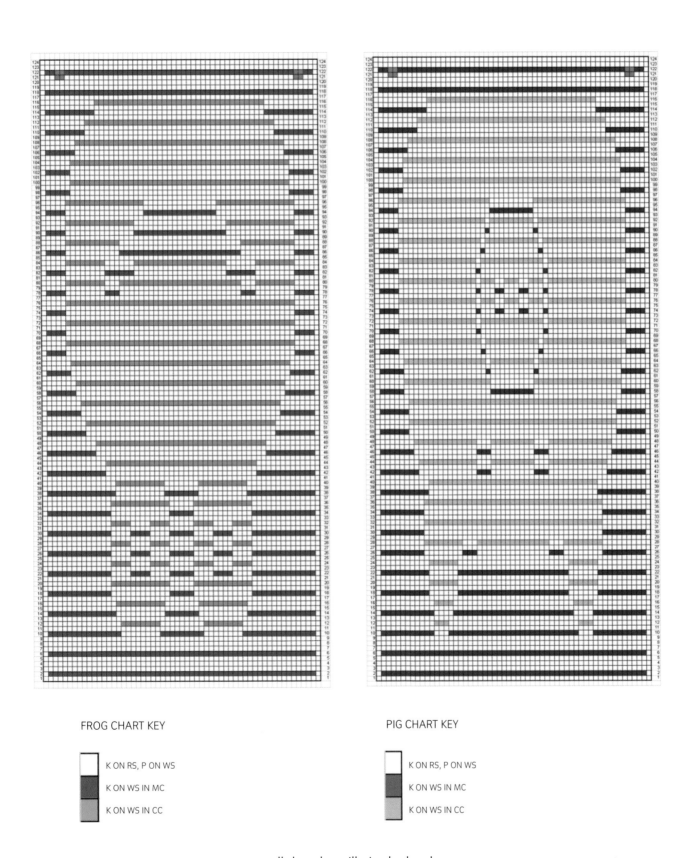

FROG CHART KEY

- K ON RS, P ON WS
- K ON WS IN MC
- K ON WS IN CC

PIG CHART KEY

- K ON RS, P ON WS
- K ON WS IN MC
- K ON WS IN CC

carry-all chameleon: illusion backpacks

diff'rent strikes
bowling ball & pins

VICKIE HOWELL • **LEVEL:** *playdate*

My little strikers love to bowl! So much so, that I've often contemplated constructing an alley in my apartment. I decided, however, that a better idea would be to knit up a toy bowling set that's durable enough for the kids to play with during the day, and soft enough for them to cuddle up with at night.

yarns

Crystal Palace Iceland (100% wool, 109 yd per 100g ball)

3 to 5 balls (for 6 to 10 pins) Color 1058, Snow White

1 ball Color 008, Red Cerise

1 ball Color 1058, black

needles

1 set (4) double-pointed needles (dpns), US Size 10½ (6.5mm), *or size needed to maintain correct gauge*

notions

Polyester fiberfill

Tapestry needle

Dried beans or lentils

GAUGE

13 sts and 15 rows = 4 inches

FINISHED SIZE

Pin: 9½ inches tall, 5 inches wide

Ball: 13½-inch circumference

directions

BOWLING PIN (MAKE 6 TO 10)

The base is knitted working back and forth in garter stitch on 2 double-pointed needles as follows:

With white, CO 3 sts. K 2 rows.

Next row: K1, M1, k to last st, M1, k1. K 1 row. Repeat these 2 rows until you have 9 sts.

K 2 more rows.

Next row: Ssk, k to last 2 sts, k2tog. K 1 row. Repeat these 2 rows until 3 sts remain.

Leaving those 3 sts on needle, pick up 4 more stitches around edge of the circle just knitted (7 sts around ⅓ of circle). With second needle, pick up 7 more sts around next ⅓ of circle edge. Using

the third needle, pick up the last 7 sts around to end of the circle (21 sts). K1, pm for beg of rounds. Knit 2 rounds.

Inc rnd: On first needle, *k1, M1, k to last st, M1, k1. Repeat from * on remaining 2 needles (27 sts).

Repeat inc rnd 3 more times (45 sts).

K even on all rnds until piece measures 3 inches from base.

Repeat inc rnd (51 sts). K 2 rounds even.

crafty tip

Stuff bowling pin while knitting to accommodate the decreases and cinching off at the end.

Dec rnd: *K2tog, k to last 2 sts on needle, k2tog; repeat from * on remaining 2 needles (45 sts).

K 2 rnds straight. Remember to stuff as you shape the pin.

Repeat dec rnd 4 more times (21 sts). K 3 rounds even. Drop white; attach red and knit 3 rows. Cut red.

Continuing with white, knit 2 more rows.

Repeat inc rnd twice (33 sts). K 5 rows even.

Repeat dec rnd 4 times until 9 sts remain. Finish stuffing, draw working yarn though remaining stitches and draw top closed. Weave in yarn end.

BOWLING BALL (MAKE 2 HALVES)

With black and set of 4dpn, CO 42 sts. Distribute stitches evenly over 3 needles and join, being careful not to twist.

K all rounds until piece measures 2 inches.

Next round: K2, *k2tog, k2; repeat from * to end (32 sts).

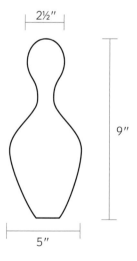

---

crafty tip

For pins that stand up better, stuff the bottom of each one with dried beans or lentils, then add polyester stuffing for the rest of the pin.

Next round: K2tog to end (16 sts).

Repeat last row until 4 sts remain. Cut yarn and draw through remaining stitches to close hole.

FINISHING

Using white and the backstitch (see page 16) embroider "Lucky" or child's name onto one half of the ball and the faux finger holes onto the other half. Stitch the two pieces together, creating a ball shape and leaving an opening to stuff. Stuff ball; sew closed.

2½"

9"

5"

square pegs
mitered square blocks

KAREN BAUMER • LEVEL: *playdate*

These blocks were inspired by my friend Sarah, who mused aloud that she loved the idea and the look of knitted blocks, but hated the idea of all the seaming they required. These require minimal sewing, and since the ends are inside the block, they need only be secured with a quick stitch or two on the inside before insertion of the foam cube.

MATERIALS (FOR THREE 4-INCH BLOCKS)

yarn

Crystal Palace Yarns Iceland (100% wool; 109 yd per 100 g ball):

1 ball each of 3 colors of your choice. Colors in blocks shown are: 8095, French Blue; 9628, Periwinkle; 0022, Pumpkin; 9660, Violet; 1240, Limeade; 1219, Fuchsia; 7243, Picnic (variegated); 7245, Seafoam (variegated)

needles

1 pair straight needles, US Size 10 (6mm), *or size needed to maintain correct gauge*

notions

Tapestry needle

Three 4-inch cubes of high-density foam

Small safety pins (optional)

~~~~~~

GAUGE

14 sts and 28 rows = 4 inches in garter stitch (k every row)

directions

SQUARE 1

With color A, CO 31 sts.

Row 1 (WS): K14, sl1, k2tog, psso (double decrease made), K14.

Row 2 (RS): K14, p1, k14.

Row 3: K13, double decrease as before, k13.

Row 4: K13, p1, k13.

Row 5: K12, double decrease, k12.

Row 6: K12, p1, k12.

Row 7: K11, double decrease, k11.

Row 8: K11, p1, k11.

Continue in this fashion, working a double decrease at the center of every WS row and purling the center st of every RS row until 3 sts remain, ending with a RS row. Double decrease on the 3 remaining sts and fasten off.

SQUARE 2

With color B, CO 16, then, with RS facing, pick up 15 sts along one edge of Square 1 (31 sts on needle). Work another square just like the first. You now have a rectangle: two squares that are attached along one edge.

crafty tip

You may find it easier to follow the instructions if you keep track of which square is finished in which order as you go along. One easy way to do this is to pin 1 safety pin on Square 1, 2 safety pins on Square 2, and so on.

SQUARE 3

With RS facing and color C, pick up 31 stitches all along 1 long edge of the rectangle. Work another square as before. (At this point your work is becoming three-dimensional.)

SQUARE 4

With RS facing and color A, pick up 31 sts along the long edge formed by Squares 3 and 2, in that order. Work another square as before. This square should be positioned on the opposite face of the cube from Square 1.

SQUARE 5

With RS facing and color B, pick up 31 sts along the long edge formed by Squares 3 and 4, in that order. Work another square as before. This square should be positioned on the opposite face of the cube from Square 2.

SQUARE 6

With RS facing and color C, pick up 31 sts along the long edge formed by Squares 5 and 4, in that order.

Row 1 (WS): K14, double decrease, k14.

Row 2 (RS): K14, p1, k13, slip 1, pick up one stitch through the edge of the square next to the one you are currently making (i.e., the edge of Square 2), psso.

Continue in this manner, working this square just as you did the previous ones, but always slipping the last st on RS rows, picking up a st from the edge of the adjacent square, and passing the slipped st over the picked up st. (As you are working your way up the final square, you are also attaching it to another square along one side; this eliminates one seam from your finishing process.)

FINISHING

Upon completion of Square 6, you will have a cube with 2 adjacent edges open. Weave in yarn ends, insert foam, and sew the cube shut from the outside, using mattress st (see page 15).

Blocks may be lightly steamed from the outside after completion to help define edges and make faces lie flat. Hold steam iron directly above each face of the cube, not quite touching fabric.

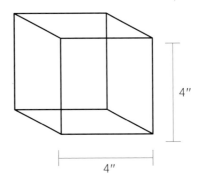

square pegs: mitred square blocks

mr. roboto
robot jammie bag

VICKIE HOWELL • **LEVEL:** *weekend at nana's*

When I was a little girl, my mom made pajama bags for all of my friends on the block. They were dolls with plastic heads and long knit dresses that acted as cozies for our sleepwear. As an adult, I realize that it was her own brilliant way of motivating us to fold our jammies. I'm hoping that my own version will work the same parenting magic with kids today that hers did more than twenty-five years ago.

MATERIALS

yarn

Berroco Quest (100% nylon; 82 yd per 50g ball):

4 balls Color platinum

1 ball Color Lapis

1 ball Color Lacquer

needles

1 pair straight needles, US Size 8 (5mm), *or size needed to maintain correct gauge*

notions

Tapestry needle

Sewing needle

Sewing thread to match Lacquer yarn

8-inch length of floral or jewelry wire

Polyester fiberfill

GAUGE

19 sts and 19 rows = 4 inches

FINISHED SIZE

21 inches tall (including antennae)

directions

FRONT BODY

With platinum, CO 45 sts. Work in St st for 8½ inches. BO.

BACK BODY PANELS (MAKE 2)

CO 26 sts. Work in St st for 8½ inches. BO.

HEAD

CO 29 sts. Work in St st for 10 inches. BO.

FRONT MECHANICAL PANEL

With Lapis, CO 31 sts. Work in St st until piece measures 6 inches. BO. Using platinum, embroider in duplicate stitch (see page 15) small rectangular "buttons" in 3 rows of 5 columns on the front of piece as shown. Sew front panel to center of front body.

LEGS (MAKE 2)

With platinum, CO 60 sts. Work in St st for 2½ inches.

RS row: BO 13 sts, k to end.

WS row: BO 13 sts, p to end (34 sts).

Continue working in St st until piece measures 8 inches from beg. BO.

ARMS (MAKE 2)

CO 28 sts. Work in St st for 5 inches. BO.

mama tip

This project makes a great gift for kiddies. Stuff it with a cozy pair of pj's and they'll never suspect that it's a practical present in disguise.

robot jammie bag

SHOULDER BANDS (MAKE 2)

With Lacquer, CO 4 sts. Work I-cord (see page 12) for 6 inches. BO.

ANTENNA

With Lacquer, CO 4sts. Work I-cord for 8 inches. BO.

FINISHING

Block all pieces.

Fold head piece in half and seam sides. Using the chain stitch (see page 16), embroider eyes, nose, and mouth onto face side of head. Fold arm and leg pieces in half; seam edges together, leaving tops open for stuffing. Stuff head, legs, and arms.

Pin front and back body together, overlapping the back body panels about an inch to create a small flap to keep the jammies from falling out of the bag; seam outer edges.

Sew arms and legs in place.

With sewing thread, tack I-cord shoulder bands into place.

Thread wire through I-cord antenna, bend in half, and shape into a loop. Sew antenna onto center of head.

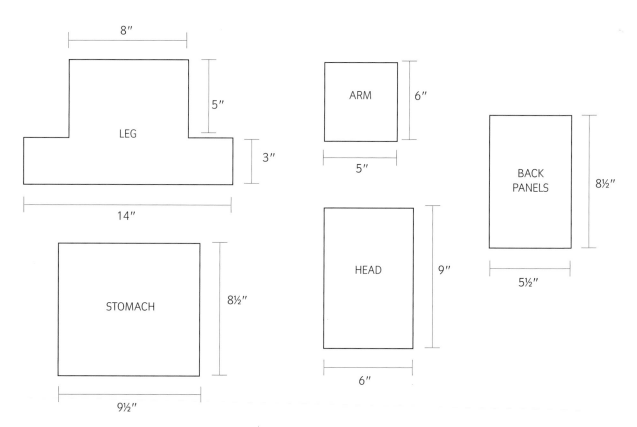

like an egyptian
egyptian dress-up

VICKI SQUARE • **LEVEL:** *summer camp*

In the land of make believe, I was always the Egyptian Queen. I have loved Egyptian art and antiquities as far back as my childhood memories go. The colors of faience and carnelian framed in gold come alive in this costume with collarpiece, head circlet, and bracelets. The tunic is meant to emulate the Egyptian gauze sheath. Top it all off with a headdress of instant hair, and your little one will soon be surveying her domain!

MATERIALS

yarn

Cascade Sierra (80% pima cotton, 20% wool, 191 yd/175m per 3½ oz/100g hank) for tunic:

3 hanks Color 01, white (MC1) AND

Cascade 220 (100% Peruvian highland Wool 220 yd/201m per 3½ oz/100g hank) for wig:

2 hanks Color 8555 black (MC2) AND

Cascade Pima Tencel (50% Cotton, 50% Tencel, 109yd/100 m per 50g ball) for jewelry:

2 balls Color 0258 Gold (CC1)

1 ball Color 7478 Carnelian (CC2)

1 ball Color 1694 Lapis (CC3)

1 ball Color 7013 Faience (CC4)

needles

1 pair straight needles US Size 10½ (6.5mm)

Two 24-inch circular needles in US Size 5 (3.75mm) and US Size 6 (4.25mm)

1 set (4) of double-pointed needles (dpn) in US Size 5 (3.75mm)

or sizes needed to maintain the various correct gauges

Crochet hook Size K (6.5mm)

notions

Tapestry needle

GAUGE

Tunic: 12 sts and 20 rows = 4 inches in garter stitch with white Sierra large (straight) needles

Headpiece top wig: 11 sts and 20 rows = 4 inches in garter stitch with 2 strands black on large (straight) needles

Headband: 24 sts = 4 inches with Tencel on small (dpn) needles

Collar piece: 8 sts = 4 inches in pattern stitch with Tencel on smaller circular needle (this is a flexible piece)

SIZE

One size fits average 6- to 8-year old

FINISHED MEASUREMENTS

Tunic: about 28 inches long, shoulder to hem, and 28- to 30- inches chest circumference

Headdress circlet circumference: about 21 inches

Hair braids: about 9 to 10 inches long

"Jeweled" collarpiece: 12½ inches at neck and 4 inches wide

Bracelets: 7½ to 8 inches around

new knits on the block

directions

TUNIC (MAKE 2)

With white (MC) and large straight needles, CO 44 sts. Knit in garter stitch (knit every row) until piece measures 21 inches. BO 7 sts at beg of next 2 rows for armholes (30 sts). Continue in garter st until piece measures 25½ inches from beg, or 4½ inches from armhole bind-off rows. Knit 9 sts for first shoulder, BO center 12 sts for neck, k9 for rem shoulder. Knit on 9 sts of rem shoulder until piece measures 28 inches from beg, or 2½ inches from neck bind-off row. BO all sts. Attach working yarn to neck edge of other side and knit to correspond.

FINISHING TUNIC

With RS tog, pin tunic pieces at shoulders. With crochet hook, slip stitch shoulder seams. Turn tunic RS out. Sew side seams from RS, using invisible weaving stitch for garter stitch, beg at underarm and working toward hem, leaving 7 inches open for side slit.

COLLAR PIECE

Starting at outer rim of collar with Gold (CC1) and larger circular needle, CO 152 sts. Change to smaller circular needle and k 1 row for foundation.

Row 1: Repeat (k2tog, yo) to last 2 sts, k2.

Row 2: P2, repeat [yo, slip yo of previous row purlwise (new yo lies over top of previous row's yo), p1].

Row 3: Repeat (k1, knit both yo's by inserting needle under both strands at same time and knit them tog as one) to last 2 sts, k2.

Row 4: K 1 row (WS) for garter st ridge on RS.

Row 5: Change to Carnelian (CC2) (Dec row on RS): K2tog, yo, k3tog, yo; rep from * to last 2 sts, k2 (122 sts).

Rows 6 and 7: Rep rows 2 and 3.

Row 8: P2, *purl next st on left needle along with the 2 yo's previously knit tog (below this same st) by inserting right needle from back to front under all 3 sts to p tog as one, p1; rep from * to end. Cut Carnelian.

Change to Gold. Knit 2 rows.**

Change to Lapis (CC3) and rep dec row (Row 5), ending k2 (98 sts). Rep from ** to **. Cut Lapis.

Change to Faience (CC4) and rep dec row to last 3 sts, k2tog, k1 (78 sts). Rep ** to **. Cut Faience.

Change to Carnelian and rep dec row to last 3 sts, ending k2tog, k1 (62 sts). Rep ** to **.

Change to Gold and rep rows 1 through 3. BO all sts as to knit.

END OF COLLAR PIECE

With gold and small dpn pick up 19 sts along side edge. Turn; BO all sts as to knit. Rep for other side edge of collar piece. Weave in all yarn ends.

TWISTED CORD TIES

Cut 3 pieces Gold each 18 inches long. With tapestry needle, thread all 3 pieces halfway through neck corner of collar piece Twist all 9-inch strands until tightly twisted. Fold at halfway point, letting collar piece hang, and let cord twist onto itself. Tie overhand knot close to end of cord. Repeat for opposite neck corner of collar piece.

HEADDRESS HAIR

Braids: With black and large straight needles, cast on 40 sts. BO. Cut, leaving 6 inches for finishing, and pull through last loop to secure. Make 54 braids.

TOP WIG

Using 2 strands black held together and large straight needles, cast on 10 sts. K 1 row. Next row: Work a bar increase into first st, k to end. Rep last row until you have 20 sts. Knit even until piece measures 4 inches from beg. K2tog at beg of next and every following row until 10 sts rem. BO all sts.

FINISHING COLLAR PIECE

Block braids, top wig, and collar piece. Lightly steam only the seams of the tunic.

HEADBAND

With color gold and small dpns, cast on 120 sts. Divide sts evenly onto 3 needles. Join, being careful not to twist cast-on edge. P 2 rows. K until piece measures 1 inch from beg. P 2 rows. BO.

Steam block from WS of headband to flatten; lightly steam from RS. Let dry.

HEADBAND FACING

With CC1 on size 5 dpn, cast on 110 sts. Join, being careful not to twist cast-on edge. K every rnd for 1 inch. BO.

EMBROIDERY FINISHING FOR HEADBAND

Cut 2 strands of Lapis, each a little over a yard long. Thread tapestry needle and make French knots (see page 16) centered vertically on headband, covering every sixth st around band. Cut 2 strands Carnelian same length and work a French knot into every other space between Lapis knots. Repeat with Faience filling in remaining spaces between Lapis knots.

FINISHING HEADDRESS

Pin top wig to top edge of headband with garter stitch ridges of top wig running front to back on

head. Whipstitch pieces tog from WS, catching purl ridge of headband and very edge of top wig. Mark center front and mark 3¼ inches on each side of center. Attach braids from side marker around back to side marker as follows: Thread one cut end into tapestry needle and insert into the purl bar lowest on WS of headband. Tie the 2 ends of braid in square knot. Repeat in every other st around headband. Attach a second layer of braids 1 purl bar up on WS of headband, between first row of braids on back half of head only. Hair then will look fuller on back side of head. When all braids are tied on, take the 2 ends of each of 2 adjacent braids and tie them together for security; repeat around.

When all braids are tied to one another a second time, cut yarn ends 1 inch long. (These ends will be hidden inside the facing piece of the headband.) Pin facing piece with purl side out, covering WS of headband and tucking all cut braid ends into facing. Whipstitch top and bottom edge of facing onto headband, catching the purl bars on the WS of the headband. You can control the head circumference measurement of the headband by how tightly you stitch the facing on.

BRACELET (MAKE 2)

With Gold on small dpn, cast on 40 sts. Divide sts onto 3 needles. Join, being careful not to twist cast-on edge. (K 1 row, p 1 row) 3 times (3 garter st ridges made). K 2 rows. Rep (k 1 row, p 1 row) 3 times. BO.

EMBROIDERY FINISHING FOR BRACELETS

Cut 2 strands Lapis each a little over a yard long. Thread tapestry needle and make French knots in St st center of bracelet, covering every fourth st around. Rep process with Carnelian for second bracelet.

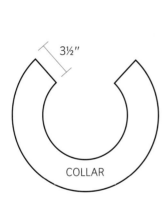

3½"

COLLAR

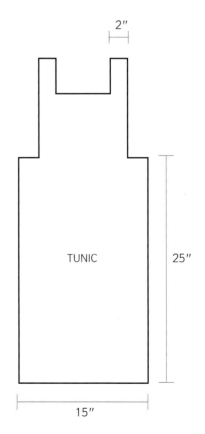

2"

25"

TUNIC

15"

splash
mermaid dress-up

TINA MARRIN • LEVEL: *summer camp*

As a child I sooo wanted to be a mermaid. They are princesses of the undersea with their graceful movements and their long gossamer hair trailing in a slow wave motion. And I grew up in what you would call a "Koi family" . . . that is, our family was and IS really IN to Koi fish (fancy Japanese Carp); complete with clubs, competitions, and endless talk of Tancho's, Kohaku's, and Ochiba's (Koi varieties). Also, as fate would have it, I have only water signs in the significant places of my astrological chart. So with all these water influences, it doesn't surprise me that the theme has crept into my knitting designs.

yarn

Schachenmayr Goa (60% viscose, 40% polyamide, 1.75 oz/50g balls):

10 balls in Color 70, Fresh

needles

1 pair each straight needles, US Size 8 (5mm) and US Size 6 (4.25mm), *or size needed to maintain gauge*

1 set (4) double-pointed needles (dpn), US Size 8 (5mm), *or size needed to maintain gauge*

Crochet hook, Size G (4.25mm)

Yarn needle

notions

Tapestry needle

GAUGE

20 sts and 27 rows = 4 inches

SIZE

One size fits children's size 5 to 6 years

FINISHED MEASUREMENTS

Top (tube part only): 7 inches long by 10 inches wide (unstretched)

Skirt: 34 inches long (including tail) by 10 inches wide (unstretched)

directions

BUTTERFLY PATTERN STITCH

Multiple of 10 sts, plus 9.

Rows 1, 3, 5, 7, and 9 (RS): K2, *sl 5 wyif, k5; repeat from * to last 7 sts, sl 5 wyif, k2.

Rows 2, 4, 6, and 8: Purl.

Row 10: P4, *on the next st (at center of slipped group) reach behind work to RS and with tip of right needle pick up 5 loose strands, and transfer them onto left needle, purl the 5 strands and the next st together as one st, p9; repeat from *, ending last repeat with P4.

Rows 11, 13, 15, 17, and 19: K7, *sl 5 wyif, k5; rep from *, end sl 5, K7.

Rows 12, 14, 16, and 18: Purl.

Row 20: P9, *pick up 5 loose strands as before, transfer to left needle and purl them together with next st, P9; repeat from *.

Repeat rows 1 through 20 for pattern.

For this pattern, the 20-row pattern repeat is called a "set." Where the pattern stitch is used, the directions list only the number of "sets" of the stitch pattern to make instead of row-by-row instructions.

note: The pattern is extremely stretchy and meant to cling like mermaid skin, so please do not be alarmed by its small size once completed. Also, the weight of the finished skirt is tolerated and more evenly distributed because of the cling factor. I know at this point I'm supposed to say "take time to check gauge," but the pattern is extremely size versatile (I, an adult woman, fit into the top pretty comfortably, so don't go nuts trying to match the gauge absolutely exactly). The skirt and top were designed with only one seam for simplicity. The top seam can be worn on the side or the back, but you need to decide which before attaching the shoulder straps. The skirt seam can be worn on the side, slightly forward, or completely back, depending on how the tail will be carried around, played with or modeled.

TOP

Cast on 99 sts with smaller straight needles.

K1, p1 rib for 6 rows.

Change to larger straight needles and work in pattern stitch for 3 sets.

Change to smaller straight needles and work in k1, p1 rib for 5 rows.

BO loosely.

shoulder straps for top (make 4)
With dpns, Co 2 sts and make an I-cord 8 (see page 12) inches long (unstretched).

SKIRT

Starting at tail fin with larger straight needles, cast on 74 sts.

Rows 1, 3, 5, 7: *K2, p7, repeat from *, end with a k2.

Rows 2, 4, 6: *P2, k7, repeat from *, end with a p2.

Row 8: *P2, k2tog, k5, repeat from *, end with a p2 (66 sts).

Rows 9, 11, 13, 15: *K2, p6, repeat from *, end with a k2.

Rows 10, 12, 14: *P2, k6, repeat from *, end with a p2.

Row 16: *P2, k2tog, k4, repeat from *, end with a p2 (58 sts).

Rows 17, 19, 21, 23: *K2, p5, repeat from *, end with a k2.

Rows 18, 20, 22: *P2, k5, repeat from *, end with a p2.

Row 24: *P2, k2tog, k3, repeat from *, end with a p2 (50 sts).

Rows 25, 27, 29, 31: *K2, p4, repeat from *, end with a k2.

Rows 26, 28, 30: *P2, k4, repeat from *, end with a p2.

Row 32: *P2, k2tog, k2, repeat from *, end with a p2 (42 sts).

Rows 33, 35, 37, 39: *K2, p3, repeat from *, end with a k2.

Rows 34, 36, 38: *P2, k3, repeat from *, end with a p2.

Row 40: (Note: This row is different from above decrease rows.) P2, k2tog, k1, *p2, k3, repeat from * for next 10 stitches, p2tog, *k3, p2, repeat from * for next ten stitches, k1, k2tog, p2 (39 sts).

Work even in stitch pattern for 6 sets. Do not turn work at end of last row.

With WS still facing you, cast on 60 sts (99 sts).

Turn work to RS and work in pattern for 7 sets more. Turn work. Change to smaller straight needles.

Next row (RS): K1, *p1, k1; repeat from * across.

Next row (WS): P1, *k1, p1; repeat from * across. Repeat last 2 rows for 7 more rows, ending with a RS row.

Next row (WS): Purl 99 sts for turning ridge.

11th row: Work in k1, p1 rib as before for 8 rows, ending with a WS row.

BO all stitches loosely in rib.

Leave a long yarn tail for seam.

FINISHING

top
Seam sides. Attach the shoulder straps as follows: Lay the top flat, with either the front or back facing you. Sew on straps 2½ inches in from side edges on front and back. Weave in yarn ends.

skirt
Seam side. Weave in yarn ends.

With 2 dpns, make a 2-stitch I-cord 35 inches long (unstretched).

Thread I-cord through purl loops on WS of turning ridge to make a belt. Fold under half of the top ribbing at turning ridge. Sew bound-off edge of top hem in place, leaving hem ends open to tie cord ends to fit waist.

With crochet hook, work single crochet (see page 17) around curling bottom edge of garment (this lessens the curl and makes a more attractive edge) and around curling edge of tail fin (not entire tail, since curling on the tail gives it dimension and increases the illusion).

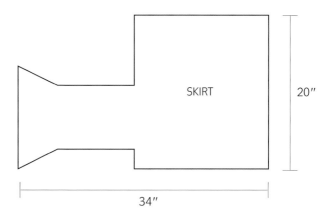

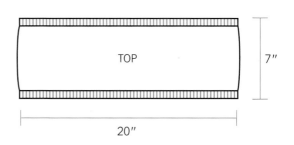

knight rider
chain mail dress-up

VICKIE HOWELL · **LEVEL:** *weekend at nana's*

No matter how technologically advanced our society becomes, the legends of the Knights of the Round Table and Joan of Arc remain magical among children. My own little warriors, who valiantly battle using knitting needle swords and yarn helmets to make the world a better place, inspired this project.

MATERIALS

yarn

Crystal Palace Soiree (60% metallic polyester, 40% polyamide, 160 yd per 50g ball):

4 balls Color 3690 (MC) AND

Berroco Suede (100% nylon, 120 yd per 50g ball):

1 ball Color 3729, Zorro (CC)

needles

1 pair each straight needles, US Size 10½ (6.5mm) and US Size 9 (5.5 mm), *or sizes needed to maintain the correct gauges*

Crochet hook, Size K (6.5mm)

notions

Tapestry needle

1-inch metal button

GAUGE

13 sts = 4 inches in MC and garter stitch, using larger needles

18 sts = 4 inches in MC and garter stitch, using smaller needles

SIZE

One size fits ages 3 to 5 years

FINISHED MEASUREMENTS

Chest armor: 16 by 22 inches (stretches to about 19 by 28 inches)

Belt: 44 by 1¾ inches

Hood: 11 inches high

directions

FRONT

With MC and larger needles, CO 46 sts. Work 6 rows in garter stitch (knit every row).

Next row: K1, *yo, k2tog; repeat from * to last st, k1. Repeat this row until piece measures 12 inches (slightly stretched).

Armhole shaping: Next RS row: BO 6 sts, k1 (at left from BO) *yo, k2tog; repeat from * to last st, k1.

WS: Repeat last row (34 sts).

Next row: K1, *yo, k2tog; repeat from * to last st, k1.

Repeat last row for 3 inches more.

Split-neck shaping: Next RS row: Continue in pattern as established in previous rows until you have 17 sts on right needle. Attach 2nd ball of yarn; with new yarn work to end (beginning with a yo). Working each side with its separate yarn; continue in pattern in this manner for 4 inches more. BO.

crafty tip

With a little help from a math program or calculator, the chest armor portion of this project can be easily adapted into a disco-style tank top for an adult!

knight rider: chain mail dress-up

BACK

Work as for front excluding the split-neck shaping. Instead, after binding off for armholes, continue in established pattern on 34 sts for 7 inches. BO.

FINISHING

With wrong sides together, seam sides. Starting from outer (armhole) edge, seam 1½ inches of each shoulder. Cut 18-inch length CC and lace it through the two sides of the split neck, working through the natural holes created by the pattern stitch.

With CC and crochet hook, work single crochet (see page 17) edging around armholes (about 39 sts).

BELT

With CC and larger needles, CO 10 sts. Work in garter stitch until piece measures 44 inches from beg. BO. Add tasseled fringe of desired length (see page 13).

HOOD (MAKE 2)

With MC and smaller needles, CO 41 sts. K 13 rows.

Row 14: K4, yo, k2tog, k to end.

Rows 15 through 23: Knit.

Row 24: BO 10 sts, ssk, k to last 2 sts, k2tog (29 sts).

Row 25: Knit.

Row 26: Ssk, k to end (28 sts).

Row 27: Knit.

Row 28: Ssk, k to last 2 sts, K2tog (26 sts).

Row 29: Knit.

Row 30: Ssk, k to last st, M1, k1 (26 sts).

Row 31: Knit.

Row 32: Repeat Row 30.

measurements are before stretching

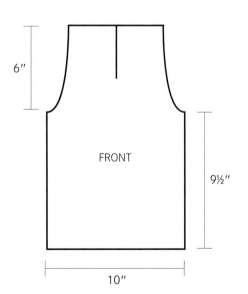

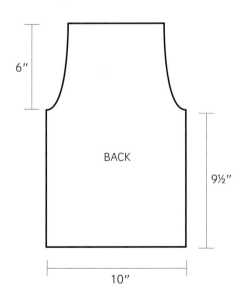

Rows 33 through 35: Knit.

Rows 36 and 37: K to last st, M1, k1 (28 sts).

Rows 38 through 49: Knit.

Row 50: Repeat row 36 (29 sts).

Row 51 through 66: Knit.

Row 67: K1, M1, k to last 2 sts, k2tog (29 sts).

Rows 68 through 70: Knit.

Row 71: Repeat row 67.

Rows 72 through 74: Knit.

Row 75: Repeat row 67.

Rows: 76 through 78: Knit.

Row 79: Repeat row 67.

Row 80: Knit.

Rows 81 through 84: repeat rows 79 and 80 twice.

Row 85: K to last 2 stitches, k2tog (28 sts).

Row 86: Knit.

Rows 87 through 92: Repeat rows 85 and 86 three times (ending with 25 sts).

BO.

FINISHING
With wrong sides together, seam back of hood. Sew on button. With crochet hook and CC, crochet single crochet in every other stitch along the bottom edge of hood (about 60 sts).

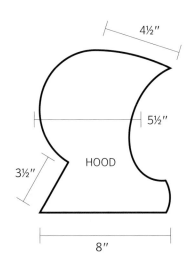

knight rider: chain mail dress-up

north shore
hawaiian dress-up

DEB WHITE • LEVEL: *weekend at nana's*

It all started one day when my daughter (then about four and a half) said, "Mommy, can you knit me a costume? A special one? Like no one else has?" Back and forth we went, drawing the pieces and trying to come up with "just the right thing." And so was born the Hawaiian Princess costume, and my daughter's undying respect and conviction that "my Mommy can knit anything." Unfortunately, now that she is six, she wants a hockey net and a pair of ruby slippers! Back to the drawing board . . ."

yarn

A: (Used for skirt) Berroco Suede (100% nylon, 120 yd/111 m per 50g skein);

1 (2, 2, 3) skeins Color 3714, Hopalong Cassidy

B: (Used for second lei, skirt, flower) Berroco Lullaby (87% Dupont Tactel nylon, 13% nylon, 126 yd/116 m per 50g skein):

1 (1, 2, 2) skeins Color 4308, Paddy Wack pink

C: (Used for skirt, bikini top) Berroco Lullaby (87% Dupont Tactel nylon, 13% nylon, 126 yd/116 m per 50g skein):

1(1, 2, 2) skeins Color 4304 Willy Winky blue

D: (Used for first lei, second lei, flower, wristlets) Berroco Crystal FX (100% nylon,146 yd/135 m per 50g skein):

1 skein Color 4707, Kryptonite green

1 skein Color 4709, Noisette beige/gold

1 skein Color 4705, Alexandrite purple

1 skein Color 4708, Kir pink

E: (Used for flower) Berroco Hush (100% nylon, 52 yd/48 m per 50g skein):

1 skein Color 6308, Paddy Wack pink

F: (Used for second lei) Berroco Hush (100% nylon, 52 yd/48 m per 50g skein):

1 skein of Color 6304, Willy Winky blue

needles

1 pair each straight needles, US Size 6 (4.25mm), US Size 7 (4.5mm), and US Size 10 (6mm). For lei, you may wish to use a longer circular needle to hold all the sts.

16-inch circular needle, US Size 6 (4.25mm)

Two double-pointed needles (dpn) for I-cord

Crochet hook, Size 7, H, or I (4.5 to 5.5mm)

notions

Tapestry needle

Three buttons, ⅞-inch diameter

Sewing needle and thread

Hair clip or barrette for flower

Elastic thread, if desired

---

note: Some yarns are used for several different pieces of the project. If you are making only a few pieces, not the whole outfit, check the yarn list AND the directions for the pieces to determine which yarns and colors are needed and determine how much of each color you will need for your chosen pieces.

GAUGE

note: Different pieces of this project have different gauges.

First lei and wristlets: 16 sts and 22 rows = 4 inches with largest needles, working in St st.

Second lei: 19 sts and 27 rows = 4 inches with medium-sized straight needles in St st.

Skirt: 26 sts and 30 rows = 4 inches (slightly stretched) with smallest straight needles in k1, p1 rib OR 26 sts and 24 rows = 4 inches (slightly stretched) on smallest straight needles in color-work ribbing.

Bikini top: 19 sts and 26 rows = 4 inches on smallest straight needles in St st; knit every rnd on circular needle (gauge may vary with St st on straight versus circular needles).

SIZE
2 (4, 6, 8) years

FINISHED MEASUREMENTS
Chest: 21 (23, 25, 27) inches

Waist: 21 (23, 25, 27) inches (garment can sit a bit lower on hip)

directions

FIRST LEI (28–30 INCHES LONG)

With 3 strands of D (the sample uses one strand each of purple, hot pink, and beige, but you can use 3 strands of the same color) and largest straight needles or circular needle, loosely cast on 96 (130) sts.

Row 1: Separate each stitch into the 3 strands, and knit one stitch into each strand [288 (390) sts].

Row 2: Knit in each of 288 (390) sts.

Row 3: Cut two of the strands, leaving one color you wish to highlight. Bind off with this one strand purlwise.

Shape the necklace into a spiral with your hands. Using the same yarn as for bind-off, sew the ends together to make a round.

SECOND LEI (28–38 INCHES LONG)

With 1 strand of B and medium straight needles, loosely cast on 115 (157) sts.

Row 1: Knit in front, back, and front again of each st (345 (471) sts). Cut yarn.

Row 2: With 1 strand of D in purple, k in each of 345 (471) sts. Cut yarn.

Row 3: With 1 strand of F, bind off purlwise.

Shape the necklace into a spiral with your hands. Using the same yarn as for bind-off, sew the ends together to make a round.

SKIRT

The waistband is knitted first. With smallest straight needles and 1 strand of A, cast on 21 (23, 25, 27) sts.

Row 1: *K1, p1; repeat from * to last stitch, k1.

Repeat row 1 for 3 (3, 5, 5) more times.

Work ribbed colorwork as follows:

Attach C.

Row 1: *K1 with A, p1 with C (carrying unused yarn on the wrong side at all times), repeat * to last st, k1 with A.

Row 2: *P1 with A, K1 with C (carrying unused yarn on the wrong side at all times), repeat from * to last st, p1 with A.

Repeat rows 1 and 2 for 7 (8, 9, 10) times more.

Cut C.

Now work in plain ribbing.

Row 1: With A only, k1, p1, repeat to last st, k1.

Row 2: P1, k1, repeat to last st, p1.

Repeat these two rows 6 (6, 7, 7) times more.

RIBBED COLORWORK SECTION 2
Attach B.

Row 1: *K1 with A, p1 with B (carrying unused yarn on the wrong side at all times), repeat * to last stitch, k1 with A.

Row 2: *P1 with A, k1 with B (carrying unused yarn on the wrong side at all times), repeat from * to last st, p1 with A.

Repeat rows 1 and 2 for 7 (8, 9, 10) times more.

Cut B.

Work plain ribbing for 16 (18, 20, 22) rows.

Continue working the sections for the waistband as follows:

4 (4, 6, 6) rows plain ribbing

16 (18, 20, 22) rows colorwork with A and C

14 (14, 16, 16) rows plain ribbing

16 (18, 20, 22) rows colorwork with A and B

14 (14, 16, 16) rows plain ribbing

16 (18, 20, 22) rows colorwork with A and C

14 (14, 16, 16) rows plain ribbing

16 (18, 20, 22) rows colorwork with A and B

14 (14, 16, 16) rows plain ribbing

12 (16, 12, 10) rows colorwork with A and C

BUTTONHOLE BAND
For all sizes: with A, and RS facing you, k 1 row.

Rows 2 and 3: *K1, p1, repeat from * to last st, k1.

Row 4: K1, p1, k1, p1, turn work; k1, p1, k1, p1, turn work; k1, p1, k1, p1, turn work; k1, p1, k1, p1. Cut yarn.

Reattach yarn just before stitch 5. *K1, p1; repeat from * for total of 6 (7, 8, 9) sts.

Turn work; **rib as just established over these 6 (7, 8, 9) sts, turn work; repeat from ** twice more. Cut yarn.

Reattach yarn at the 11th (12th, 13th, 14th) stitch. *K1, p1; repeat from * for total of 6 (7, 8, 9) stitches, turn work; ***rib as established over these 6 (7, 8, 9) sts, turn work; repeat from *** twice more. Cut yarn.

Reattach yarn at the 17th (19th, 21st, 23rd) stitch. K1, p1, k1, p1, k1, from *, turn work; k1, p1, k1, p1, k1, turn work; k1, p1, k1, p1, k1, turn work; k1, p1, k1, p1, k1. Do not cut yarn.

Next row: *K1, p1*, repeat from * to * to last st, k1. Repeat for another 2 rows. Bind off purlwise.

These row counts will yield waist measurements of 21 (23, 25, 27) inches.

FINISHING

Weave in all the ends. Wet block, if necessary. Sew on buttons to correspond to the buttonholes and desired waist measurement.

FRINGE

Cut 30 (32, 28, 42)-inch lengths of A, B, and C or as desired (noting that each strand is double the finished length). To attach each strand: Fold one strand in half exactly. Insert the crochet hook from back to front at the desired spot. Draw folded end through to make loop. Slide ends of strand through loop and pull tight. You will need one strand for every 2 knitted rows along the bottom edge. For plain ribbing sections, use A. For colorwork ribbing sections, use the contrast color in the ribbing. Trim ends evenly. The skirt buttons over the left front hip.

FLOWER (TO ATTACH TO CLIP FOR HAIR OR TO SEW TO CLOTHES)

Using medium straight needles and B, cast on 8 stitches, leaving a long end for sewing.

stamens

*In same st, k in front, back, front, back, front and back loop (6 sts in one), slip first st just made (the one farthest from needle tip) over all the other 5 sts on right needle; repeat with second, then third, and so on, until only 1 st remains on right needle. Starting with that st, bind off all stitches on left needle until only 1 st remains**.

Using knit-on cast-on (see page 22), CO 7 sts (8 sts now on needle)***.

Repeat from * to *** once more, then repeat from * to ** once (3 stamens made). Cut yarn, leaving a long end.

petals

With E, make petals as follows:

*CO 7 sts (total of 8 now on needle).

Row 1: For this and every odd-numbered row, knit (8 sts).

Row 2: Knit to last st, knit in front and back loop of that one stitch (9 sts).

Row 4: Knit to last st, knit in front and back of that one stitch (10 sts).

Row 6: Knit to last 2 sts, k2tog (9 sts).

Row 8: Knit to last 2 sts, k2tog (8 sts).

Row 9: BO all stitches but the last one.

Repeat twice more (3 petals made). Cut yarn.

LEAVES

Using Crystal FX in green, *CO 7 sts (total of 8 now on needle). Knit 2 rows. Bind off 6 sts (2 sts left on needle).

Knit 2 rows. Repeat from * twice more (3 leaves made). BO the remaining two sts.

Starting with the stamens, roll the flower so that the leaves are on the outside. Sew through all thicknesses firmly, leaving two long ends of B to attach the flower to something (such as a hairclip or barrette).

WRISTLETS (MAKE 2)

Using 3 strands of Crystal FX (I used green, gold/beige, and hot pink) and smallest straight needles, cast on 5 sts. Knit in reverse St st (p on RS, k on WS) until band is about 5 (5¾, 6, 6½) inches or long enough to fit wrist. Bind off. Sew bound-off edge to cast-on edge and weave in yarn ends.

BIKINI TOP

Using yarn C and circular needle, cast on 100 (112, 124, 136) sts; join to work in rounds, being careful not to twist the stitches.

First 3 rounds: Work in k1, p1 ribbing.

Then continue in plain St st (k every rnd on circular needle) until piece measures 3 (4, 5, 6) inches from beg. Work in k1, p1 ribbing for last 3 rounds. Bind off loosely in ribbing.

FINISHING

If desired, run some elastic thread through the top and bottom of the piece.

for the tie

With C and 2 dpn needles, CO 3 sts and work a 6- to 8-inch length of 3-stitch I-cord (see page 12). Tie the finished cord in a knot around the center front of the top, bunching the fabric together.

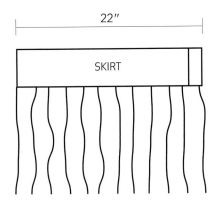

22"

SKIRT

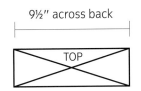

9½" across back

TOP

18½" circumference
(stretches to 21")

north shore: hawaiian dress-up

i am the warrior!
viking dress-up

VICKI SQUARE • **LEVEL:** *summer camp*

When I visited the National Museum in Dublin, I had the exciting pleasure of seeing a Viking longboat and many other artifacts associated with the fierce warriors. As a costume I couldn't resist the Viking helmet with horns. My felted version is sturdy enough for any young master of make-believe. The tunic has "leather" strips laced together, and "fur" hides for shoulder armor. Gold torque bracelets accent the true Viking ensemble, and complete the image. A more ferocious pint-sized warrior you will never see!

MATERIALS

yarn

Cascade 220 (100% Peruvian highland wool, 220 yd/201 m per 3½ oz/100g hank):

3 hanks Color 9446, burgundy (MC1)

1 hank Color 7822 (CC1)

1 hank Color 4010 (CC2) AND

Berroco Suede (100% nylon, 120 yd/111m per 1¾ oz/50g ball):

3 balls Color 3714 (MC2) AND

Crystal Palace Splash (100% polyester, 85 yd/77 m per 100g ball):

1 ball Color 7185, sable (CC3)

needles

One 16-inch circular needle each, US Size 13 (9mm) and US Size 10½ (6.5mm)

1 set (4) double-pointed needles (dpns), US Size 13 (9mm)

1 pair each straight needles, US Size 9 (5.5mm) and US Size 8 (5mm), *or size needed to maintain the various correct gauges.*

notions

Tapestry needle

Small stitch holders

Long (quilting) straight pins

2 handfuls polyester fiberfill

GAUGE

Helmet: Cascade 220 with 2 strands held tog, 11 sts and 14 rows = 4 inches in St st before felting

Tunic yoke: Cascade 220 with 2 strands held tog, 17 sts and 24 rows = 4 inches in linen stitch

Tunic body: Berroco Suede 9½ sts and 14 rows = 2 inches in St st; total width of strip 19 sts = 3¾ inches

Tunic fur shoulders: Crystal Palace Splash 16 sts = 6 inches in rev St st

FINISHED SIZE

Fits an average 6 to 8 year old.

Tunic is 25 inches long shoulder to hem, ties allow for flexible chest measurement fitting 25 to 30 inches comfortably; helmet circumference is 21 inches.

LINEN STITCH PATTERN

Work on odd number of sts.

Row 1: K1, *wyif sl 1 purlwise, wyib k1; rep from * across.

Row 2: Wyib sl 1 purlwise, *wyif p1 wyib sl 1; rep from * across.

Repeat Rows 1 and 2 for pattern.

REVERSE STOCKINETTE STITCH

P 1 row, k 1 row; repeat for pattern.

directions

HELMET

Using MC1, with 2 strands held tog, and larger circular needle, CO 70 sts. Join, being careful not to twist sts. Knit even for 4 inches.

Dec row: (K5, k2tog) 10 times (60 sts). Knit even for 3 rows.

note: Change to double-pointed needles when needed as you decrease.

(K4, k2tog) 10 times (50 sts). Knit even for 3 rows.

(K3, k2tog)] 10 times (40 sts). Knit even for 3 rows.

(K2, k2tog) 10 times (30 sts). Knit even for 3 row.

(K1, k2tog) 10 times (20 sts). Knit even for 3 rows.

(K2tog) 10 times (10 sts). Cut end and draw through all remaining loops to secure.

HELMET BANDS

Use MC1, 1 strand only and smaller circular needle.

Lower band: CO 75 sts; join, being careful not to twist sts. Work reverse St st for 5 rnds. BO.

Band strips (make 4): CO 24 sts. Work back and forth in reverse St st for 4 rows. BO. Cut yarn and draw cut end through last loop to secure; then thread end into tapestry needle and make running stitch at short end of strip. Gather tightly to make point and secure. Weave in yarn ends.

HELMET HORNS (MAKE 2)

With CC1, 2 strands held tog, and larger circular needle, CO 26 sts. Do not join; work back and forth in rows. Work even in reverse St st for 4 rows.

Short row: P23, wrap and turn, k20, wrap and turn, p20, p2tog, p1 (25 sts).

*Knit to last 3 sts, k2tog, k1 (24 sts). P to last 3 sts, p2tog, p1 (23 sts). K to last 3 sts, k2tog, k1 (22 sts). *

Short row: P19, wrap and turn, k16, wrap and turn, p16, p2tog, p1 (21 sts).

Rep from * to * (18 sts).

Short row: P15, wrap and turn, k12, wrap and turn, p12, p2tog, p1 (17 sts).

Rep from * to * (14 sts).

Short row: P11, wrap and turn, k8, wrap and turn, p8, p2tog, p1 (13 sts).

Knit to last 3 sts, k2tog, k1 (12 sts).

Short row: P9, wrap and turn, k6, wrap and turn, p6, p2tog, p1 (11 sts).

Rep from * to * (8 sts).

Rep last 2 rows (6 sts).

P2tog, p2, p2tog (4 sts).

Cut yarn, leaving 18-inch tail for seam. Draw cut end through last loops to secure. Fold horn in half with WS (knit side) tog; weave seam, pulling snugly enough to encourage curve.

TUNIC

"Leather" strips: Use Berroco Suede (MC2) and smallest straight needles; CO 19 sts. Border seed st row: K1, *p1, k1; repeat from * to end. Repeat this row twice more.

Now work as follows: Next row: K1, p1, k15, p1, k1.

Next row: K1, p1, k1, p13, k1, p1, k1.

Repeat last 2 rows until piece measures 15½ inches from beg. Work border seed st row twice. BO in seed stitch pattern.

YOKE

Using MC1 with 2 strands held tog, and larger straight needles, CO 45 sts.

Work in linen stitch (see page 109) until piece measures 3 inches, ending with a RS row.

Next row: Work pattern row 2 for 15 sts; place these sts on stitch holder for right shoulder. BO next 15 sts in ribbing until 15 sts remain, counting 1 st remaining on right needle from BO. *P1, wyib sl 1 purlwise; repeat from * to end.

Work 15 sts on needle for left shoulder until piece measures 10 inches from neck bind-off, ending with a RS row. Place sts on a st holder. Transfer right shoulder sts onto needle, attach working yarn to neck edge, and continue in pattern on right shoulder sts until piece measures 10 inches from neck bind-off, ending with a WS row. Transfer left shoulder sts onto needle. With RS facing you, attach working yarn and work pattern over 15 sts of left shoulder, CO 15 sts for neck, continue pattern over 15 sts of right shoulder (45 sts). Continue in pattern until piece measures 3 inches from cast-on neck edge, ending with a WS row. BO in ribbing.

Block pieces flat, let dry.

With 3 strips side by side, pin top (short) ends of strips to bottom edge of yoke. Using a double strand of wool, whipstitch strips to yoke, catching only bound-off edge in seam.

Tunic fur shoulders: Measure and mark 12 inches down from shoulder on front, and 12 inches on back (24 inches total). Using Crystal Palace Splash (CC3) and smaller circular needles, pick up 64 sts evenly spaced along armhole between markers. Work reverse St st for 3 rows.

Next row: Work 2 sts tog at beg and end of next and every following row until fur piece measures 3 inches from armhole. BO all sts.

SIDE TIES (MAKE 4)

With MC1 and smaller circular needles, CO 40 sts. BO. Attach 1 tie to WS of each bottom corner of yoke.

TORQUE BRACELETS
(MAKE 2; FINISHED CIRCUMFERENCE ABOUT 7 INCHES)

Cut 10 strands CC2, each 24 inches long. Make twisted cord (see page 12). Tie all ends tog into large overhand knot. Trim ends even. Insert knot into folded end to form bracelet circle.

FINISHING

Mark yoke for "rivet" placement, 5 across width of yoke, 7 placed across shoulder as indicated in photo. Cut four 1½-yard lengths of CC2. Thread tapestry needle with all 4 strands. Make large French knots (see page 16), each with 2 wraps around needle for each rivet.

Machine felt (see page 15) helmet, strips, and horns. (Knit side of helmet and purl side of band, strips, and horns = RS.) Attach band to lower edge of helmet. Work French knots as for yoke at 10 points evenly spaced. Mark quarter points on helmet. With gathered end at top, attach strips to helmet at quarter points from band to top of crown with French knots at 5 points evenly spaced along each band.

Stuff handful of stuffing into horns. Pin horn at mid-point between 2 strips and sew onto helmet using overcast st with yarn to match horn. Repeat for second horn on opposite side.

TUNIC LACES

Cut two 60-inch lengths of CC1. Thread both strands through tapestry needle and insert halfway (30 inches) from WS through tunic ½ inch below yoke and centered in seed stitch border of tunic strip (on edge adjacent to center strip). Cross over to adjacent strip and insert needle to WS to form first part of *X*. Working over strip seam, make a half cross-stitch every 2½ inches down seam. Thread remaining 30-inch ends of CC1 in tapestry needle and insert from WS in adjacent tunic strip. Repeat process to complete cross-stitches to make laced seam. End with laces on WS; tie a square knot and weave in yarn ends. Repeat on seam on opposite side of center strip.

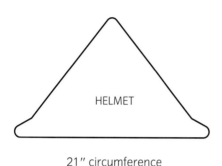

HELMET

21″ circumference

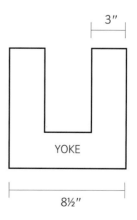

HORN

9″

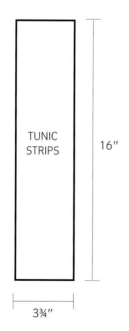

TUNIC STRIPS

16″

3¾″

3″

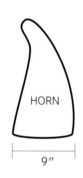

YOKE

8½″

about the
contributors

KAREN BAUMER
CROWN & MITERED SQUARE BLOCKS

Karen has been knitting since she was fourteen years old and especially loves to knit for her friends' kids. She has had designs published in several knitting books and magazines, and has appeared on the television series *Knitty Gritty*. She spends a good portion of her days making wee garb for her business, www.PhiBetaBaby.com. At last count her boyfriend had 23 hand-knit sweaters in regular rotation.

CHRISTINA BENEDETTI
UNICORN DRESS-UP

Christina's aunts taught her how to knit in the third grade, but she picked it up only occasionally throughout elementary and middle school. She didn't return to knitting until the summer of 2002, when her cousin got her hooked during a family vacation. Now she likes to design and knit things to sell at her neighborhood craft fairs. She also works at Temptations, a great yarn store in Dublin, Ohio.

BEVERLY GALESKAS
FELTED WIZARD & PRINCESS HATS

Beverly Galeskas, author of *Felted Knits* (Interweave Press, 2003) and owner of Fiber Trends Pattern Company, is well known for her felted knit designs. She has been a guest on both *Knitty Gritty* and *Shay Pendray's Needle Art Studio* and taught at many knitting conferences and yarn stores across the country.

CANDI JENSEN
FANCY DRESS

Candi has worked as a designer in the craft and needlework industries for more than twenty-five years. She has had over three hundred designs published in national magazines including *Vogue Knitting* and *Family Circle Knitting*. She has appeared on numerous television programs featuring innovative ways to use knit and crochet, including *Knitty Gritty* and the *Carol Duval Show*. She has also worked for many years in the promotional side of the industry, promoting the use of knitting and crochet through charitable organizations. She is the author of five books, *Hooked on Crochet*, *Knit Scarves*, *Candy Tots*, *Candy Blankies*, and *Candy Babies*.

Candi, known as much for her sense of humor as her color sense, lives in northern California with her husband, Tom, three cats, and a neighborhood full of children who, along with her grandson Johnny, are a constant source of inspiration.

TINA MARRIN
MERMAID DRESS-UP

Tina is an artist and knitter living in the Los Angeles area. She learned to knit while doing her masters work in art when a fellow artist needed lessons for a knitted artwork in her thesis show. So possessed was Tina with the newfound craft that she blew off her own thesis show and only displayed two artworks on the wall with a mountain of knitted hats in the middle of the room. Tina approaches most of her knitting projects in an expressionistic way, that is, just casting on and letting the piece evolve how it wants to. Tina makes anything from Braille sweaters, with bobbles as the Braille bumps, to her now famous knitted boots, which she makes by drilling into existing high heels to make holes then casting on and engulfing the shoe in knitting.

JILLIAN MORENO
TWIRLY TANK

Jillian Moreno knits and designs knitting patterns to keep her head from exploding while she's being a mama to Isobel and Henry. She sells her patterns through her Web site, acmeknittingcompany.com and is a frequent contributor to Knitty.com.

SHETHA NOLKE
ILLUSION BACKPACKS

After about five months of knitting, Shetha decided that she could master the art of illusion pattern designing. Her career in a very structured scientific environment inspired her to use spreadsheet applications to generate illusion designs easily. The combination of geek and knit is mastered in illusion knitting and this is why Shetha took to illusion knitting so well. She also enjoys Fair Isle, Aran, and all other kinds of knitting too. She mostly enjoys knitting the small, quick projects for her son, born in May 2003.

KERRIE RYCROFT
STRIPED LEG WARMERS & BAG

Kerrie lives just outside of London in the UK with her husband and two children. Having recently moved and had a baby within a few weeks, her knitting time is more limited at present than she would like. She still manages to find time most days to work on her new designs and update her Web site at www.kerriesplace.co.uk. Her four-year-old daughter has a mind of her own on most subjects including what mummy should knit for her and is quick to suggest designs / ideas that she would like to wear. Her son has yet to wear his first hand-knit sweater designed by mum but that day is fast approaching; the opportunity to experiment with boys clothes is too exciting to pass up!

VICKI SQUARE
EGYPTIAN & VIKING DRESS-UP

Vicki is a fiber artist and author of the famously popular *Knitter's Companion*, *Folk Bags*, and soon-to-be-released *Folk Hats*, all published by Interweave Press, and *Knit Great Basics*, published by Brown Sheep Co. She is passionate about her creative pursuits in fibers, designing knitted pieces from basics to unique art to wear. Magazines have featured her work, and she has won awards for her innovative designs. She regularly teaches workshops throughout the country.

LORI STEINBERG
PIRATE BATH SET

Lori directs plays and musicals in New York City. She learned to knit in the 1980s backstage with the cast and crew of the off-Broadway show she was working on as a production assistant.

DEB WHITE
HAWAIIAN DRESS-UP

Deb is an elementary school teacher with a husband, a six-year-old daughter, and a passion for knitting. She designs and knits clothes for her family and friends and has even been known to knit slipcovers for chairs. She is also an adult survivor of being dressed to entertain the neighbors. But she's over that now. Almost.

NATALIE WILSON
FIREFIGHTER HAT

From her Detroit-area base, Natalie Wilson designs for magazines, yarn companies, and her own iKnitiative line of patterns. Her various knitting exploits are documented at her Web site, www.iknitiative.com. Natalie's in-home fan club includes a terrific husband and two wonderful young children, all of whom are incredibly tolerant of her ever-growing yarn stash.

about the author

VICKIE HOWELL

A self-proclaimed crafty gRRRL, Vickie Howell has been involved in the creative arts for as long as she can remember. Before becoming the mother of two boys, she worked in the entertainment industry at companies including International Creative Management (ICM) and Alliance Atlantis Entertainment. Post motherhood, she has founded three crafty Web-based businesses and two Stitch 'n' Bitch groups. She is a proud member of the infamous Austin Craft Mafia and the host of *Knitty Gritty*, a hip and funky knitting series for the DIY-Do-It-Yourself Network. Her designs can be found in publications nationwide as well as on the new DIY television series, *Stylelicious*, which she co-hosts with the other Craft Mafia ladies. Vickie lives, breathes and knits in Austin, Texas. For more info, check out www.vickiehowell.com.

about the photographer

CORY RYAN

Cory Ryan has worked as a videographer, editor, and motion graphics artist in Austin since 2000. One creative visual medium led to another, and Cory began pursuing photography as a hobby in 2002. It quickly evolved into a love affair with her Nikon, and she has been snapping shutters ever since. Her interests have brought her a wide range of work, including fashion, portraiture, wedding, and product photography. She has since garnered kudos from brides and business owners Austin-wide. Cory is also the founder and managing director of Flicker, a local film festival spotlighting film-only projects & providing funding to the local film community. For more info, go to www.coryryan.com.

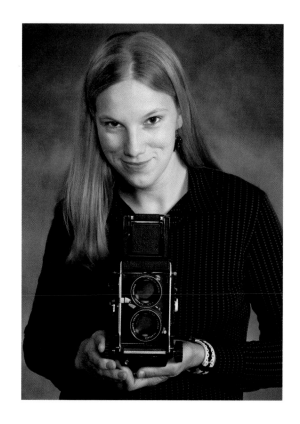

index